Professional Learning
Communities at
Work™ and # Virtual
Collaboration

On the Tipping Point of
Transformation

RICHARD DUFOUR
CASEY REASON

A Joint Publication With

Solution Tree | Press

a division of
Solution Tree

555 North Morton Street
Bloomington, IN 47404
800.733.6786 (toll free) / 812.336.7700
FAX: 812.336.7790

email: info@solution-tree.com
solution-tree.com

Visit **go.solution-tree.com/PLCbooks** to download the reproducibles in this book.

Printed in the United States of America

19 18 17 16 15   1 2 3 4 5

Library of Congress Cataloging-in-Publication Data

DuFour, Richard, 1947-
    Professional learning communities at work and virtual collaboration : on the tipping point of transformation / by Richard DuFour and Casey Reason.
        pages cm
    Includes bibliographical references and index.
    ISBN 978-1-935542-93-3 (perfect bound) 1. Professional learning communities. 2. Teachers--In-service training. 3. Educational technology. 4. Educational change. I. Reason, Casey S. II. Title.
    LB1731.D774 2016
    370.71'1--dc23
                                2015020849

Solution Tree
Jeffrey C. Jones, CEO
Edmund M. Ackerman, President

Solution Tree Press
President: Douglas M. Rife
Associate Acquisitions Editor: Kari Gillesse
Editorial Director: Lesley Bolton
Managing Production Editor: Caroline Weiss
Senior Production Editor: Christine Hood
Proofreader: Jessi Finn
Text and Cover Designer: Rian Anderson
Compositor: Rachel Smith

Acknowledgments

This book was written with the heartfelt belief that we have just begun examining the impact of professional learning communities (PLCs) in schools. With the advent of new technologies and transformational tools, we believe the capacity to dramatically accelerate the power and potential of PLCs is on the horizon.

We offer sincere thanks to Dr. Barbara Hopkins and Mark Stevens of the National Education Association (NEA) and Dr. Cindy Guillaume. Their belief in teachers, the profession, the creative capacity of others, and the concepts associated with virtual collaboration helped us bring these emerging ideas to millions of teachers in building the largest PLC in the history of the profession. Thanks also to Stephanie Heald. Her early work in virtual team learning continues to mold and inspire our perspectives. Finally, Dr. Kent Scribner's belief in PLCs and the capacity to use virtual teams to mold leaders and find creative ways to solve our toughest challenges in schools helped us to shape this book and the work ahead.

This book was made possible thanks to the innovative leaders of Solution Tree. Thanks to each of you for pushing us to bring the best of ourselves to this project and for encouraging us to challenge our readers and our profession to continue to aspire to greater heights. The best is yet to come.

Visit **go.solution-tree.com/PLCbooks** to download the reproducibles in this book.

Table of Contents

About the Authors

Richard DuFour, EdD, was a public school educator for thirty-four years, serving as a teacher, principal, and superintendent. During his nineteen-year tenure as a leader at Adlai E. Stevenson High School in Lincolnshire, Illinois, Stevenson was one of only three schools in the nation to win the United States Department of Education Blue Ribbon Award on four occasions and the first comprehensive high school to be designated a New America High School as a model of successful school reform. He received his state's highest award as both a principal and superintendent.

A prolific author and sought-after consultant, he is recognized as one of the leading authorities on helping school practitioners implement the Professional Learning Communities at Work™ process in their schools and districts.

Rick wrote a quarterly column for the *Journal of Staff Development* for nearly a decade. He also was the lead consultant and author of ASCD's video series on principalship as well as the author of several other videos. He was presented with the Distinguished Scholar Practitioner Award from the University of Illinois and was the 2004 recipient of the National Staff Development Council's Distinguished Service Award.

To learn more about Rick's work, visit www.solution-tree.com.

 **Casey Reason, PhD,** is an expert in training leaders to maximize the effectiveness of teams and creating conditions for peak performance. For more than a decade, he has worked with schools all over the world in helping to implement school improvement initiatives through innovative leadership approaches, engaging teacher leadership, and establishing professional learning communities (PLCs). Casey also has consulted with numerous large corporate clients, including American Express and General Dynamics. He currently is a featured leadership scholar and is on the Executive MBA Advisory Board for Colorado Technical University. Casey is an expert and early innovator in the area of virtual learning and engagement. For more than a decade, his company has developed virtual learning experiences for clients throughout the world, and his work in virtual learning earned his company a Blackboard International Designer of the Year award in 2010, an accolade featured on Forbes.com. He also developed an innovative leadership coaching framework called BEST, which brings together school leaders from throughout the world in a creative, virtual coaching collaboration and professional learning framework. Casey currently works with Solution Tree Press in developing and delivering online course offerings.

Casey's first book, *Leading a Learning Organization: The Science of Working With Others*, was endorsed by the best-selling author of *The One Minute Manager*, Dr. Kenneth Blanchard. Earlier in his career, Casey was a lead content developer for Laureate Learning Systems Inc. and the inaugural chair for doctoral leadership studies at Grand Canyon University. At age thirty, Casey became the principal of Whitmer High School, one of the largest urban schools in Ohio. At the time, Whitmer was on the verge of being rated as in academic emergency. After five years of reform, Whitmer received a special commendation for rapid growth and improvement from the Ohio Department of Education. Casey later applied these principles at the district level as an assistant superintendent for instructional services in Northville, Michigan.

Casey earned a PhD from Bowling Green State University and lives with his sons, Brice and Kiah, in Scottsdale, Arizona.

To learn more about Casey's work, visit www.caseyreason.com, or follow him on Twitter @CaseyReason.

To book Rick or Casey for professional development, contact pd@ solution-tree.com.

Introduction

We were purposeful in selecting the subtitle of this book. Malcolm Gladwell (2002) describes the "tipping point" as that magic moment when an idea, trend, or social behavior crosses a threshold and spreads like an epidemic. We are convinced that educators may be at the tipping point of transforming education because of the combined power of the Professional Learning Communities at Work™ (PLC at Work™) process and the opportunity to expand and enhance that process through technology. Numerous robust examples of virtual collaboration exist today, but our profession has only scratched the surface of what is possible when educators infuse the power of technology with the transformative elements of the PLC process.

In high-performing PLCs, educators:

- Focus on the critical questions that must be addressed in schools that profess a mission to ensure learning for all students
- Collaborate with one another to improve their professional practice
- Take collective responsibility for student learning

- Use evidence of student learning to inform and improve their professional practice

- Develop systems of intervention and enrichment to meet the needs of all students

Technology and virtual teaming have already had a positive impact on the PLC process in a number of schools. Before collaborative team meetings, teachers use technology to access timely information on student learning. During the meetings, teachers go to the web to find answers to questions or to initiate a critical conversation with a colleague who may only be known to them in cyberspace. With technology and virtual teaming, team members access assessment items from other teachers or from assessment experts and connect to links that illustrate effective instructional strategies. They watch informative videos and participate in dynamic blogs and threaded discussions that contribute to the school's ever-growing shared knowledge. At no point in history have teachers had the ability to learn so much from so many.

Technology has certainly created the potential for richer and deeper team dialogue. Educators must, however, expand on and make more strategic use of the power of technology if deeper learning is to become the norm for collaborative teams. The good news is that conditions have never been more favorable for using technology as a catalyst for improved professional practice.

The Potential of PLCs to Redefine a Profession

The PLC process has helped to redefine the role of educators from isolated individuals in isolated classrooms to collaborative teams of colleagues working collectively to solve problems. The culture of schooling is slowly changing to recognize that:

> The idea that a single teacher, working alone, can know and do everything to meet the diverse learning needs of thirty students every day throughout the school year has

rarely worked, and it certainly won't meet the needs of
learners in years to come. (Carroll, 2009, p. 13)

The evidence of the impact of collaboration among teachers and
schools continues to accumulate. Case studies, such as those found
at www.allthingsplc.info, provide examples of schools and systems
with at least three years of sustained PLC work and measurable
impacts on student results. Studies of the world's best school systems
find that these systems organize their schools into PLCs (Barber &
Mourshed, 2009; Mourshed, Chijioke, & Barber, 2010). Syntheses
of meta-analyses, such as those provided by John Hattie (2012),
demonstrate that collaboration is not merely a congenial activity
but rather a process for improving both student and adult learning.
There is now compelling evidence that effective collaboration at the
individual, school, and system levels leads to better student results
and higher professional satisfaction by teachers and leaders.

Technology as a Catalyst for Improvement

Technology has become ubiquitous in the 21st century. There are
now more handheld devices in the world than there are toothbrushes
(Hopkins & Turner, 2012). Dental hygiene notwithstanding, it is
undeniable that thanks to technology, contemporary educators have
greater access to transformational tools than any generation pre-
ceding them. It is also evident that technology has the potential to
change how schools work (Chandler, 2012). As most futurists and
technology experts predict, we are still very much in the throes of
this transformative evolution (Bonk, 2010; Van Dusen, 1997).

Furthermore, the youngest generation of educators entering the
profession today is uniquely accustomed to using technology as part
of its normal routines. For example, the millennials, roughly defined
as those entering the workforce just after the turn of the century
(Howe & Strauss, 2000), are more likely to communicate with their
friends through texts or instant messaging than a phone call. They
download their music rather than going to music stores. They avoid

standing in line for movies and stream them instead. They search online for dating partners. While previous generations polished their shoes and nails in hopes of making a good first impression, millennials polish the presentation of their dating profiles or their Facebook pages. They turn to the Internet when they have questions or want advice on hotels, restaurants, cars, doctors, electronics, appliances, and weekend activities. Millennials often seek five to seven pieces of advice or feedback from different Internet sources prior to making a decision (Burstein, 2013). Most of those offering advice are unfamiliar to them and, in many cases, are responding from a different country from those seeking information. People of this generation are primed to use the power of technology to enhance their professional practice because they have used technology in almost every aspect of their lives.

Millennials are not, however, the only ones embracing technology. In 2014, Facebook had an estimated one billion users, and Twitter had 271 million. From 2012 to 2014, Facebook's fastest-growing demographic was users ages forty-five to fifty-four. Their presence on Facebook jumped by 46 percent. In that same time period, Twitter experienced a 79 percent growth in users ages fifty-five to sixty-four (Pew Research Center Internet Project, 2014).

Beyond these social media tools, the ubiquity of high-powered handheld devices; the emergence of video inputs over text; and the instantaneous access to unlimited amounts of information have forever changed how people of all ages engage in both work and play. Technology has become a part of the daily lives of virtually *all* Americans and can help reshape and ultimately accelerate the work of PLCs. The tipping point will occur when the conductivity, speed, and access to learning enjoyed by some educators are embraced and utilized by the masses. The best time to begin this transformation is now.

Technology as an Accelerating Force

In the decade since Thomas Friedman (2005) declared that the world is flat, we've learned quite a bit about the advantages of technology as well as its potential for missteps and overreach. If educators learn to leverage technology tools in a strategic manner to support continuous school improvement powered by the PLC process, schools can be transformed for the better. What's important to keep in mind is that technology, in its many forms, is not the destination. Instead, it's an accelerating force in helping to pursue the innovations that make a difference.

Even though technology has become such an integrated part of our lives, there is still a lot to learn about its most efficient applications. To that end, it's important to study ongoing, bold, creative attempts to use technology and the powers to connect and learn from innovative thought leaders who are trying to refine what we know about virtual teaming and collaboration. One such interesting exemplar of experimentation was born from the National Education Association (NEA). In 2014, the NEA launched an experimental learning and collaboration platform called the Professional Practice Communities (formerly known as Great Public Schools). The goal of this endeavor was to create an almost limitless community of passionate practitioners who could come together and find meaningful collaborators to inspire classroom-ready innovations essential to the profession. These efforts were driven by the creation and support of virtual teams from across the nation, which came together and identified best practice solutions to some of education's most difficult challenges. Using the ideas presented in this book, Casey trained more than seventy teacher leaders from throughout the United States to facilitate this unique learning community. Their mission was to proudly establish the largest-ever virtual PLC. By all accounts, they were successful in this endeavor, hosting at one point as many as ten thousand active teacher-innovators working together online in an attempt to showcase the power of frontline change and improvement coming directly from the ranks of passionate teaching professionals. This is just one example of the many steps educators are taking today to use technology more thoughtfully. This book aims to inspire more creative experiments and identify the best practice approaches to establishing new and innovative connections.

Raising the Bar

Individual and collective human performance has always been impacted by the performance of others. In 1954, Roger Bannister became the first person to run a mile in under four minutes. Previously, many had considered a sub-four-minute mile humanly impossible. Soon after Bannister proved that theory wrong, many other runners duplicated his feat, and the four-minute barrier tumbled (BBC Online, 1954). Human beings hadn't suddenly gotten faster. The gravitational pull hadn't been minimized. Instead, a more powerful shift had occurred: people changed their assumptions about what was possible. Once people have evidence that goals and tasks are being accomplished in an irrefutably better way someplace else, they believe that achieving at higher levels is a possibility.

Educators in PLCs use actual evidence of student learning to identify outlier teachers, teams, and schools—places where more students are consistently learning at higher levels than the norm. Once we identify these outliers and hold up their professional practices and results for consideration, we present educators with an opportunity to observe, study, seek help from, and imitate these modern-day Roger Bannisters.

Virtual collaboration allows the profession to expand this practice exponentially. The highest-performing middle school mathematics teacher in a building may find that there are other teachers a county, a country, or even a continent away doing significantly more with less. Used effectively, this virtual collaboration could help even the best teachers engage in their own Roger Bannister moment. With the expansion of virtual collaboration, teachers everywhere can redefine their own standards for what is possible.

Enhancing Depth of Engagement

Many readers of this book have experienced the confusion of being entirely unsure whether a recent communication with a friend or colleague was done face to face, through email, through text message, or via some other current message-sending tool. This is because using technology has become so commonplace. Critics may condemn its lack of face-to-face interaction, but text messages, emails, Twitter, Voxer, and other forms of electronic communication have allowed us to increase the immediacy of interaction and break down barriers of time and space. While quantity does not necessarily equal quality, the enhanced capacity to connect with others can accelerate a school's ability to identify problems, find solutions, and correct mistakes. The availability of technology, virtual teams, and access to expertise outside of school provides educators with an opportunity to build a more sustainable culture for adult learning.

Meeting the Challenges of Contemporary Times

We recognize that these may be some of the most difficult days our profession has ever faced. Educators today must grapple with the highest expectations for student achievement in our history at the same time they are confronting obstacles and challenges that previous generations could not have imagined. We contend, however, that educators also have access to opportunities that were never available to the generations who preceded them. If today's educators stay true to the PLC process—with its emphasis on working collaboratively rather than in isolation—and make strategic use of the technology tools available to them, the opportunity for unprecedented results may be on the horizon.

The fundamental building block of the PLC process is a collaborative team structure that supports shared learning, collective responsibility, action research, and continuous improvement. Virtual teams can extend shared learning, expand collective responsibility, engage more people in action research, and serve as catalysts for continuous improvement. If done well, educators can connect with others beyond the walls of their schools and push each other to continually improve.

None of this, however, is guaranteed. Simply plugging in and connecting will not necessarily yield the most profound results. Educators must be wise enough to both remain dedicated to the foundational elements of the PLC process and take full advantage of the emergent opportunities available for reinventing the profession with new and exciting ways to connect, innovate, and transform.

Our profession is often accused of being slow to change and blind to innovations occurring beyond the school walls. However, initiating change for the sake of change, or constantly pursuing the newest innovation, has not served our profession well in the past and will not serve it well in the future. To meet the challenges of contemporary times, schools need more than tweaking at the margins of practice. They must be truly transformed. Merging the PLC process with the potential of virtual teaming, virtual collaboration, and access to greater expertise can contribute to the necessary transformation in the following ways.

Strong Teams

Teaming with an emphasis on collective responsibility is at the heart of the PLC process. The strategies utilized in developing virtual teams and the investment in conceptualizing all the various aspects of virtual conductivity should ultimately contribute to the development of more deeply engaged, interconnected, committed, and effective teams. While the accessibility of shiny handheld devices and the efficiency of cogently designed collaborative spaces are helpful conduits to the process, virtual teams, virtual conductivity, and all the tools and tips shared in this text are designed to make teams stronger and more impactful in meeting the challenges of the day.

Capacity Building

As a study of the world's best school systems concludes, "The quality of an education system cannot exceed the quality of its teachers . . . the only way to improve outcomes is to improve instruction" (Barber & Mourshed, 2007, p. 40). Thus, the key to improved student learning in any school is to ensure the ongoing learning of the educators who serve those students. When the PLC process is embedded in the very culture of a school, an invaluable, fully accessible catalog of shared knowledge is created and continuously enhanced. When combined with virtual teaming and access to expanded knowledge bases, the PLC process creates a unique opportunity for ongoing adult learning.

School Culture

The strategies presented in this book demonstrate how the PLC process, the use of virtual teams, and increased opportunities to connect can have a positive impact on creating a more deliberately connected and consistently successful school culture. As the collaborative team structure replaces teacher isolation, and as the collective analysis of transparent evidence of student learning replaces the privatization of teaching practice, the culture is changed in profound ways. As using technology to seek information and support from both within school and outside of school becomes the norm, the tradition of closing one's classroom door to create a cloistered world gives way to a culture in which giving and receiving support are seen for what they are—profoundly professional.

The Learning Ahead: Chapter Overview

Chapter 1 places the PLC process in historical context, demonstrates the growing interest in PLCs, and highlights problems educators might encounter when attempting to implement the process. This chapter reviews traditional assumptions that have shaped school culture and stresses the importance of embracing new assumptions to foster cultural change. We emphasize the fact that using technology is not a magic elixir to guarantee school improvement, acknowledge research that identifies common problems encountered by virtual teams, and share strategies for addressing those problems.

Chapter 2 stresses the most pertinent question virtual teams should ask themselves—not whether they are collaborating but rather what they are collaborating *about*. Virtual collaboration is a means to an end, not the end itself. This chapter clarifies the essential issues that must drive the efforts of virtual teams committed to the PLC process.

Chapter 3 introduces three strategic levels for establishing effective virtual teams in a PLC. Most of the chapter focuses on the first level—engineering a strategic e-connection. It presents and explains the ten dimensions for engineering a strategic e-connection that are often overlooked when initiating virtual teams.

Chapter 4 addresses the second strategic level for establishing effective virtual teams in a PLC by offering strategies for e-collaboration that can help educators avoid some of the technical and personal problems that arise with electronic collaboration. Many of these strategies remind educators about the importance of the affective side of teaming.

Chapter 5 illustrates the third strategic level for establishing effective virtual teams by offering suggestions for enhancing learning with e-acceleration. Essential to this level is openness to sharing problems with and learning from an audience that goes far beyond the team. It reviews the ten dimensions for engineering a strategic e-connection from chapter 3 when applied to a commitment to open sourcing.

Chapter 6 offers suggestions for organizing and orchestrating effective teams, whether they are virtual or face to face. It illustrates how effective teams can approach their work in ways that increase the likelihood of success.

Chapter 7 presents a case scenario of a high school committed both to the PLC process and to using technology to enhance the power of that process. It explains how this school approaches the challenge of integrating technology into the routine work of its collaborative teams and the benefits that result.

Chapter 8 addresses the nature of leadership necessary to support both school-based and virtual teams. It presents five keys to effective leadership and specific strategies for bringing those keys to life. Servant leadership, dispersed leadership, loose-tight cultures, reciprocal accountability, and situational leadership are some of the concepts that are addressed in this chapter.

Finally, chapter 9 concludes the book by offering a medical analogy, which asserts that the key to effective use of technology and collaboration to support the PLC process is a change in mindset regarding the fundamental approach to our profession.

Conclusion

The most powerful factor in support of student learning has always been, and always will be, a highly effective classroom teacher. The challenge facing schools is how to ensure more effective teaching in more classrooms more of the time. The best solution to this challenge is to create the conditions in which teachers are constantly learning how to improve their craft and enhance their individual and collective capacity through a learner-focused, collaborative, results-oriented culture provided by the PLC process. This book demonstrates how establishing coherent systems for organizing, managing, and supporting virtual teams can enhance the power of this process.

Our most important goal, however, is to persuade educators that our profession has the opportunity to transform education in meaningful ways that are both desirable and feasible. We do not consider the ideas in this book to be utopian. In fact, we believe these ideas represent strategies for transforming education that are powerful, pragmatic, and already proven in practice by many schools. We do not claim that bringing these ideas to life more strategically for the majority of educators will be easy. Significant achievements never are. But it is time for our profession to aspire to more, to dream bigger. As Michelangelo (n.d.) once wrote, "The greater danger for most of us lies not in setting our aim too high and falling short; but in setting our aim too low, and achieving our mark."

CHAPTER 1

Examining the Past to Understand the Present

Nothing is stronger than an idea whose time has come. For nearly 150 years, this paraphrase of Victor Hugo's writing has reminded us of the power of compelling ideas. Imagine, however, if two forceful ideas whose time has come merged in a synergistic way to create the potential for a combined impact that is greater than the sum of both ideas. We have arrived at that fortunate convergence in education with growing evidence of the power of PLC at Work and the use of technology as a catalyst for organizational improvement and individual and collective learning.

Technology can enhance the PLC process both within school walls and beyond. Educators now have the capacity to create powerful *virtual collaboration* that can exponentially expand their access to expertise beyond their team, school, or district. Membership in the collaborative teams that drive the PLC process need no longer be restricted to educators assigned to the same building. Easy access to technology does not, however, guarantee that the technology is used productively. Virtual collaboration may never realize its full potential to impact professional practice unless those who engage in that collaboration embrace the key tenets of the PLC process. Conversely, the PLC process is unnecessarily limited without the benefits that technology can provide.

A Quick Definition

We will go into much greater detail about the characteristics of PLCs and virtual collaboration later in the book, but we feel a quick explanation is warranted here. What is a *PLC*? When schools or districts operate as PLCs, educators engage in an ongoing process of working collaboratively in recurring cycles of collective inquiry and action research in order to achieve better results for the students they serve. Note that the larger organization—the school or district—represents the PLC. *Collaborative teams* of educators are the fundamental building blocks of the PLC structure and the engine that drives the PLC process.

Virtual collaboration is designed to help educators use technology to extend, enrich, and ultimately improve on the existing PLC process. When done well, virtual collaboration applies the power of technology to:

- Improve communication

- Enrich collegial relationships

- Extend opportunities for innovation

- Expand access to professional expertise

- Promote best practices in supporting student learning

- Accelerate the learning of individual educators and collaborative teams

Which teachers could benefit from virtual collaboration? We offer the following partial list.

- A singleton teacher who represents the only person in the building who teaches a particular subject, course, or grade level

- Small teams of teachers looking to expand the number of members contributing to the work of their teams

- Teachers who believe teaching, like all professions, requires a constant search for best practices

- Teachers who have a burning passion for their subjects and want to deepen their knowledge with other like-minded colleagues

- Teachers willing to share their knowledge, skills, and strengths with others in order to increase their impact on students' lives

- Teachers willing to model the commitment to lifelong learning they hope to instill in their students by engaging in an ongoing study of the art and science of their craft

- Teachers confronting challenges they have been unable to resolve

- Teachers who believe that the craft knowledge and experience of practitioners represent a powerful resource in improving instruction and solving problems

- Teachers who recognize the benefits of expanding their access to practitioner expertise beyond their team, building, or district

- Teachers who would like to contribute to addressing and overcoming the challenges of the profession

- Teachers who, like Henry Adams (2008)—historian, journalist, novelist, and educator—recognize that "a teacher affects eternity; he can never tell where his influence stops" and, thus, hope to expand their influence beyond the students in their classrooms

In short, we contend that *all* teachers could benefit from virtual collaboration. Those who cannot benefit from collaboration should benefit from a change of career.

School Improvement Efforts

Yale psychologist Seymour Sarason (1996) devoted much of his work to examining the culture of schools and the problem of change. He summarizes his findings with this terse sentence:

> If you want to change and improve the climate and outcomes of schooling both for students and teachers, there are features of the school culture that have to be changed, and if they are not changed, your well-intentioned efforts will be defeated. (p. 340)

This observation has been echoed repeatedly by those who have devoted their professional lives to school improvement (Barth, 2001; Fullan, 2013; Johnson & Kardos, 2004; Louis & Wahlstrom, 2011; McLaughlin & Talbert, 2006; Newmann & associates, 1996; Schlechty, 1997; Timperley & Robinson, 2001).

By *culture*, we mean the typically unexamined assumptions, beliefs, attitudes, expectations, and behaviors that constitute the norm for people throughout the school or organization. Educators in every school have a culture, but in a very real sense, the culture of the school has them. Culture defines the work of the school and shapes the way people go about doing the work, and it simply becomes "the way we do things around here."

Some of the cultural traditions in schooling that have stalled efforts to improve teaching and learning include:

- A professional norm of teachers working in isolation

- The belief that teaching constitutes transmitting knowledge to relatively passive students; therefore, it is the teacher's job to teach—it is the student's job to learn

- The expectation and belief that some students will not and cannot learn

- The assumption that the purpose of schools is to sort and select students into different programs based on their aptitudes and likely careers

- The conviction that decisions regarding curriculum, instruction, and assessment should be made by those outside the classroom and carried out by teachers with fidelity

To examine the origins of these assumptions, let's consider conditions in the United States at the turn of the 20th century.

Traditional School Culture

As the 19th century came to a close, the combined forces of the Industrial Revolution, urbanization, and immigration had fundamentally changed the United States. Cities grew as immigrants poured into the country, and labor forces congregated around factories that required hundreds or thousands of hands working in unison on strategically assembled, process-driven assembly lines. This shift from a rural economy to the factory model resulted in work environments driven by time. Bells and whistles signaled workers to stop or start certain actions. A strict division between managers and workers was created. Managers were to identify the one best way to complete a task and then establish and enforce standardization of work methods. Workers were considered incapable of understanding the work process and, thus, simply did as they were told.

Frederick Taylor (1911), a leader in establishing this approach to efficiency, referred to it as *scientific management*. Other historians referred to it as *Taylorism* after Taylor himself. Schools were not immune to the pervasive influence of Taylor's scientific management. Ellwood Cubberley (1919), one of the most distinguished educators in the United States during this period, argued that schools should prepare students to work in the factory environment.

Later, he articulated the parallels between Taylor's scientific management in industry and the task of schooling. Cubberley (1919) writes:

> The public schools of the United States are, in a sense, a manufactory, doing a half-billion dollar business each year in trying to prepare future citizens for usefulness and efficiency in life. As such we have recently been engaged in applying to it some of the same principles of specialized production and manufacturing efficiency, which control in other lines of the manufacturing business. (pp. 378–379)

The impact of scientific management on education can still be seen today. In many schools, bells signal the start and end of instruction; the minutes of seat time for students are monitored carefully; and teachers are told by "experts" far removed from the classroom what curriculum to teach, which instructional strategies to use, how to pace content, and how to assess student learning. District leaders are expected to discover the "one best way" to ensure student learning, and teachers are to perform the tasks with fidelity.

A Gradual Shift in School Culture

By the 1990s, some educators had begun to reject Taylorism and embrace the ideas of W. Edwards Deming (n.d.), who called for leaders to help establish a clearly defined and consistent purpose for their organizations, break down barriers between management and workers, encourage frontline problem solving, and create systems of continuous improvement. Although vestiges of Taylorism remain clearly evident in many organizations today, current employers assert that they are looking for employees who have the capacity to work with others, collaborate, problem solve, and create (Blanchard, Cuff, & Halsey, 2014).

The PLC movement has extended some of Deming's ideas of defining a clear and constant purpose (learning for all students), creating a collaborative culture in which those closest to the action (teachers) play a major role in decision making, and developing systems to constantly monitor and continuously improve the process (teaching and learning). Taylorism no longer rules in PLCs.

Need some examples? Taylorism requires people to work in isolation. The PLC process requires that people work together. Taylorism demands close supervision of workers, assuming they can't be trusted. The PLC process empowers teachers to make important decisions and allows for innovation and creativity in teaching. Taylorism calls for a top-down hierarchy, with managers dictating the one best way to accomplish a task. The PLC process relies on widely distributed leadership and engages everyone in the organization in a constant search for best practices through ongoing collective inquiry. Taylorism champions uniformity. The PLC process encourages action research and using evidence of student learning to identify and share each teacher's individual strengths for the betterment of the team.

One of the greatest contrasts between Taylor's theories and the PLC process is the very purpose of schooling. Taylor believed that schools should sort and select students according to their innate abilities. Educators were to identify the small percentage of people capable of being managers and provide for their ongoing education to prepare them for the responsibilities they would assume. Great masses were to be trained to work compliantly in the industrial setting with the minimum education necessary for manual labor.

PLCs operate from the assumption that schools must ensure *all* students learn at high levels and are prepared to continue learning throughout their lifetimes if they are to meet the demands of the 21st century. Rather than sorting and selecting according to perceived abilities and assumed occupations, members of PLCs strive to ensure that all students learn by identifying what is most essential for them to learn, monitoring each student's learning on an ongoing basis, creating processes to ensure they receive additional time and support when they struggle, and using evidence of student learning to continuously improve professional practice.

In short, the PLC process calls long-standing assumptions about schooling into question, embraces a fundamentally different purpose for schools, and asks educators to redefine how they go about doing their work. The process acknowledges the craft knowledge of teachers and is based on the premise that *all* teachers, not just a few representatives, should be engaged in thoughtful consideration of curriculum, pacing, instruction, assessment, and planning for improvement.

The Rise of PLCs

Many veteran educators have become skeptical of educational innovation because, time and again, they have seen those innovations fall victim to a predictable life cycle. The innovation is launched with great fanfare and early enthusiasm. As inevitable difficulties arise and educators recognize that the new program does not provide the answers to all their problems, enthusiasm wanes. The innovation becomes buffeted by the strong winds of criticism and disenchantment. Within a few years, it is cast adrift into the vast sea of failed reform initiatives as school and district leaders go in search of the next new thing. It is no wonder that educators respond to calls for school improvement with a resigned "This too shall pass." They have been conditioned to do so.

The PLC process avoids this traditional pattern. In the late 1980s and 1990s, interest in and exploration of the process was generally limited to researchers rather than practitioners. Around the turn of the century, however, the idea of PLCs began to make inroads in a growing number of schools. By 2005, Rick DuFour and colleagues Rebecca DuFour and Robert Eaker were hosting PLC summits and institutes sponsored by Solution Tree, which drew in thousands of teachers and administrators eager to learn more about the process. At this early juncture, they polled the audience on two questions: (1) How many of you work in schools that organize staff into collaborative teams that work interdependently to achieve common goals directly tied to improved student learning? and (2) How many of you are provided with time each week to collaborate with your colleagues?

Even though these are just the first small structural steps on the PLC journey, few attendees responded in the affirmative. In the summer and fall of 2014, DuFour, DuFour, Eaker, their colleague Mike Mattos, and dozens of other PLC at Work associates asked those same questions of more than twenty-five thousand educators from throughout the United States and beyond, attending the PLC summits and institutes. More than 80 percent indicate that these structures are in place in their schools.

This anecdotal evidence certainly doesn't reach the standard of research, but there are other indicators we can identify that suggest interest in the PLC process continues to grow rather than diminish. Virtually all professional organizations for educators—teachers and administrators—endorse the PLC process and urge their members to contribute to transforming their schools into PLCs. Researchers around the world have concluded that the PLC process offers the greatest potential for improving schools. An international study of teaching and learning affirms the positive impact of the PLC collaborative culture not only on student achievement but also on educator self-efficacy and job satisfaction (Organisation for Economic Co-operation and Development [OECD], 2014b). As the study notes, "Ample research evidence shows that a powerful movement of change takes place when teachers cooperate and work together, resulting in effective schools, classrooms, and student learning" (OECD, 2014b, p. 174). The report concludes with a call for providing teachers with more time to collaborate.

A series of studies by the McKinsey & Company research group to determine what educators could learn from the world's highest-performing school systems concludes that these systems rely on the PLC process to provide ongoing professional development essential to continuous improvement (Barber & Mourshed, 2009; Mourshed et al., 2010). (For summaries of research supporting the PLC process and endorsements of the process by professional organizations, refer to "Finding Common Ground in Education Reform: Professional Learning Community Advocates—A Presentation of the Research" on www.allthingsplc.info [www.allthingsplc.info/files /uploads/advocates.pdf].) Moreover, a survey of more than one hundred thousand teachers in thirty-four different countries found that teachers in the United States and other countries in the world value collaborating with colleagues and would like more time to do so (Sparks, 2014). In fact, when DuFour and his colleagues began writing about the power of the PLC process, they could point to a few model schools that demonstrated the sustainable power of the process. Today, they can point to hundreds.

When Rick and his colleagues began their work, they focused on individual schools. Today, entire districts and regions have successfully implemented the process in all their schools—and have the results to show for it. The PLC process has led to sustainable, systemwide improvement in districts throughout the United States, serving very different student populations with huge discrepancies in resources.

At this point, it is fair to say the PLC concept has avoided the rapid rise and fall of traditional school improvement initiatives. Interest in PLCs in the United States and around the world has never been greater and continues to grow.

The Problem With PLCs

Now that we have painted a rosy picture of the prevalence and sustainability of the PLC process, allow us to also acknowledge that even the most powerful concepts can be misinterpreted or badly applied. The downside of the ubiquity of the term *PLC* is the fact that the term is in danger of losing all meaning. Virtually any loose coupling of educators who share a common interest is calling itself a PLC. There is confusion regarding what constitutes a PLC—a school, a district, collaborative teams, or congenial colleagues within a school or district. We have observed hundreds of schools and districts who proudly proclaim that they are PLCs but do virtually none of the things that PLCs actually do. Some educators regard the process as a menu from which they select some elements of the process and ignore others. Others see it as a linear checklist to move through and be done with rather than a recursive process of continuous improvement for students and adults.

In some districts, teachers are removed from the collective inquiry that builds collective capacity and organizational learning. When someone else makes all the decisions—what is taught, when it is taught, how long a unit should last, what assessments are used, how student proficiency is determined—teachers are removed from the adult learning fundamental to a PLC. It is the process of working through and answering these critical questions *together* that leads to greater educator knowledge about their craft and greater commitment to their decisions.

In many instances, we have seen the desire to ensure adult comfort and convenience trump a collective effort to help more students learn. Because the PLC process calls existing assumptions into question, conflict is inevitable. Some schools choose to avoid that conflict. Because the process calls for joint analysis of transparent evidence for student learning, some schools elect to eliminate this core element of the process rather than address the anxiety that accompanies it. There may be breakthroughs on the PLC journey, but there are also brick walls, and it may appear easier in the short term to return to the comfortable ways of the past than to work through the challenges.

However, the biggest impediment to the PLC process is the tendency to view it as a program to add to the existing structure and culture of the school or district, rather than a deliberate attempt to shape a new structure and culture. The process begins with educators working together to honestly assess the current reality of their organization. They must then do the following.

- Clarify the mission they are attempting to accomplish

- Articulate a clear and compelling vision of the school they must create to achieve the mission

- Identify the collective commitments they pledge to honor in order to create such a school

- Establish the results-oriented goals they will use to mark their progress

The very foundation of the PLC process demands clarity regarding shared missions, visions, collective commitments, and goals. With that foundation in place, all members of the PLC are called on to align every practice, procedure, process, and decision with the collective purpose, direction, assurances, and aspirations of the educators in that community. Without this shared foundation, schools will continue to pursue random acts of innovation.

The Impact of Technology in the Classroom

As we asserted previously, no generation of educators has ever had more ready access to such powerful technology than contemporary teachers. Students and teachers alike have unprecedented information and expertise at their fingertips. The opportunity to create a network of educators working together to enhance their professional practice and collectively solve problems has never been greater. We should, however, once again look back before moving forward.

The idea that advances in technology can dramatically improve schools is not a new one. As one enthusiast declared, "The inventor or introducer of the system deserves to be ranked among the best contributors to learning and science, if not among the greatest benefactors of mankind" (Tyack & Cuban, 1995, p. 121). The year was 1841. The "system" to which he referred with such zeal and admiration was the blackboard.

Thomas Edison predicted "the motion picture is destined to revolutionize our educational system and that in a few years it will supplant largely, if not entirely, the use of textbooks" (Tyack & Cuban, 1995, p. 111). Advocates for radio and television also made extravagant claims regarding the impact these new technologies would have in schools. The typical life cycle for these technology-driven reforms is described as follows:

> Hyperbolic claims about how a new invention would transform education; then research showing that the technology was generally no more effective than traditional instruction and sometimes less; and finally, disappointment as reports came back from classrooms about the imperfections of the reform and as surveys showed that few teachers were using the tool. (Tyack & Cuban, 1995, pp. 121–122)

Computer companies, software companies, technophiles, and futurists have been predicting for decades that computers would fundamentally change how schools operate. Since 1980, advances in technology have certainly exceeded all expectations. A student with a smartphone has more computing power than was used to launch the *Apollo 11* spacecraft that took humans to the moon. Access to technology for teachers and students has exploded. Consider tables 1.1 and 1.2 (page 26).

Table 1.1: The Explosion of Computers in Schools

Year	Percentage of Schools With Computers	Number of Students per Computer
1981	18%	888
1989	97%	24
2000	99%	4.2

Source: U.S. Bureau of the Census, 1991, 2001.

Table 1.2: The Explosion of Access to the Internet in Schools

Year	Percentage of Schools With Internet Access	Percentage of Classrooms With Internet Access
1995	50%	8%
2000	98%	77%

Source: U.S. Bureau of the Census, 2001.

By the turn of the century, 87 percent of schools had local area networks, and four of every five classrooms had computers (U.S. Bureau of the Census, 2001).

The impact of computers on schooling, however, has fallen far short of predictions. Although many studies purport that technology improves student learning, others challenge that conclusion. One laments the fact that "it is still surprising to see how many teachers do not use technology at all" (Byrom & Bingham, 2001, p. 10). A more recent study finds that only 17 percent of teachers believe technology can help students explore their own ideas, and only 26 percent believe students apply technology to problem solving. The new generation of teachers may be comfortable using technology in their own lives, but they are teaching in a system that lags behind the times (Schwartz, 2013).

The famous five-year study of the impact of technology in Apple Classrooms of Tomorrow (ACOT) finds that access to technology improves student engagement and encourages classroom teachers to rely less on direct instruction and more on cooperative learning. The same study reports, however, that the students in these schools do no better on standardized tests than students without access to the technology and teaching reforms of the ACOT schools (Baker, Gearhart, & Herman, 1994).

Another study finds that students who use computer-assisted, drill-and-practice technologies actually perform worse on the National Assessment of Educational Progress than students who do not have access to those technologies (Wenglinsky, 1998). In 1993, Stanford University historian Larry Cuban argued that the story of computers in education could be summarized as "Computers Meet Classroom: Classroom Wins" (p. 185). Later, he asserted that computers in the classroom were "oversold and underused" (Cuban, 2001). Ten years later, a former president of the International Society for Technology in Education stated, "At present, the technological capacity available to schools exceeds our ability to use it effectively to enhance learning" (Schrum, 2010, p. 6).

As recently as 2012, a meta-analysis of forty years of research on the impact of digital technology on student achievement concluded that "taken together, the correlational and experimental evidence does not offer a convincing case for the general impact of digital technology on learning outcomes" (Higgins, Xiao, & Katsipataki, 2012, p. 3). This demonstrates a failure in building a relationship between technology applications and student performance, which may be due to the inadequacy of the technology, failure to implement it properly, or limitations of standardized tests themselves.

There are several reasons why providing widespread access to computers has not transformed schools. Expectations regarding technology's impact on learning are often unrealistic to begin with. Technology purchases are often made in the absence of clearly defined, results-oriented learning goals. Acquiring computers becomes the end in itself rather than a means to the end of enhancing student and adult learning.

Professional development has often been lacking. The infusion of computers has typically not been accompanied by the ongoing training, practice, and support teachers need to become proficient in integrating technology into instruction. In an international survey of teachers, teachers report that their greatest needs for professional development are in the combined areas of information and communication technologies and how to integrate new technologies into their classrooms (OECD, 2014b).

The evaluation of technology's impact on learning also is lacking. Standardized tests used to assess the impact of technology often require recall of information rather than the higher-order thinking skills and depth of knowledge that effectively integrated technology can promote.

Teachers may be unsure of how to use technology to develop lessons that are student centered, collaborative, engaging, and self-directed and that promote higher-order thinking skills. This kind of inquiry-based learning demands not merely an infusion of technology but also fundamental changes to curriculum, pedagogy, and assessment (Boss, 2015; Darling-Hammond et al., 2008).

However, the biggest obstacle to technology's impact on student and adult learning is inattention to the existing structure and culture of schools. If the assumptions, beliefs, attitudes, expectations, and behaviors that constitute the norm for people throughout schools remain unexamined and unchanged, technology only serves to reinforce the existing paradigm. If educators merely replace drill-and-kill worksheets with drill-and-kill computer programs, there is no reason to expect significantly better results.

We hope it is evident that we are not zealous technophiles encouraging educators to rush to acquire the latest and greatest hardware or software to hit the market. For example, one of the latest trends in the application of technology is integrating it into one's clothing and accessories (Tehrani & Michael, 2014). Google glasses and smartwatches perform the same functions as smartphones, and they are now available for those who find reaching into their pocket for their phone too much of an effort. Whether these innovations add value to the lives of users or simply serve as charming accessories is yet to be determined.

The same can be said of integrating technology into the PLC process. The way in which educators approach the concept of virtual collaboration determines whether it serves as a tool for enhancing, deepening, and strengthening the PLC process or a charming accessory that adds little value to professional collaboration.

It should be self-evident that technology is a tool—a means to an end rather than an end in itself. If technology contributes to an organization's core purpose and benefits its users, it can accelerate improvement, but it doesn't guarantee or cause improvement (Collins, 2001). Sir Francis Galton, one of the greatest scientific thinkers of the early 20th century, observed, "A rude instrument in the hand of a master craftsman will achieve more than the finest tool wielded by the uninspired journeyman" (Pearson, 1930, p. 50). The challenge facing educators is not determining the best hardware or software to purchase but rather how to develop the capacity of every educator to become a master craftsman able to utilize the potential power of technology to improve learning for students as well as adults.

Understanding Virtual Teams

The collaborative team is the core structure of a PLC and the engine that drives the entire PLC process. Creating virtual collaborative teams presents educators with both opportunities and challenges. The business world has embraced the virtual team structure for decades, providing researchers and organizations alike with opportunities to assess the advantages and disadvantages of that structure.

A survey of more than thirty thousand employees working in virtual teams for multinational companies reveals major challenges in establishing effective teams. Among the challenges identified by members of these teams are the inability to read nonverbal cues; difficulty in establishing interpersonal relationships; an absence of collegiality among members; difficulty in establishing rapport and trust; greater problems in managing conflict; greater problems in making decisions; and difficulty in expressing personal opinions.

When asked what they hope for in a virtual teammate, respondents said they value colleagues who are willing to share information, proactively engaged, collaborative, organized, capable of demonstrating good social skills, able to provide useful feedback, and willing to offer assistance (RW[3] CultureWizard, 2010).

Thus, educators must be aware that while there are many benefits to participating in virtual teams, there are also challenges that must be addressed. We address the benefits and challenges more fully in the following section.

Benefits and Challenges of Virtual Teams

A comprehensive review of the research lists the following benefits of virtual teams.

- Unite experts in specialized fields working at a distance from each other
- Provide members with the ability to tap into centers of excellence, regardless of their location
- In some instances, produce better outcomes
- Facilitate innovation and creativity
- Enable members to share their knowledge and expertise
- Offer accessibility to highly qualified people, regardless of their location

The same review also recognizes inherent challenges in the virtual team structure, including the following.

- Decrease the ability of leaders to monitor the work of teams
- Produce greater vulnerability to mistrust, communication breakdowns, conflict, and power struggles among team members
- Have difficulties identifying the appropriate technology to support the team

- Experience challenges in managing conflict when members are not in the same location

- Build assumptions and expectations based on cultural differences among organizations

- Experience difficulties in using various technologies, as some members are technophobes

- Face challenges in coordinating work

- Offer fewer opportunities for collegial interaction, often leading to weaker conceptual understanding of a problem among members

- Require special training for team members (Ebrahim, Ahmed, & Taha, 2009)

Educators who hope to enjoy the benefits of virtual teams must be aware of the challenges they will confront in implementing that structure. More importantly, they must proactively identify and adopt specific strategies for overcoming those challenges.

It's a Matter of Trust

As Stephen Covey, A. Roger Merrill, and Rebecca Merrill (1995) write, "Trust is the glue of life. It's the most essential ingredient in effective communication. It's the foundational principle that holds all relationships" (p. 203). Members of site-based teams build trust not only through their collaborative work but also through their daily, informal interactions—sharing meals, discussing personal matters, and socializing outside of work. On virtual teams, however, trust is measured almost exclusively in terms of reliability, consistency, and responsiveness (Kirkman, Rosen, Gibson, Tesluk, & McPherson, 2002; Meyer, 2010). Whereas social bonds and relationships are keys to establishing trust on face-to-face teams, predictable performance is vital to building trust on virtual teams.

Reliability and predictable performance of effective virtual teams require absolute clarity among all members regarding the purpose, processes, and routines of their teams (Watkins, 2013). Ambiguity is the enemy of any collective effort, but it is fatal to virtual teams. Members must establish a common language with shared understanding of the meaning of key terms, agree on the results-oriented goals they are pursuing, clearly define roles and responsibilities with specifics about who does what and when, establish and honor a process for making decisions, and identify benchmark targets and time lines to help monitor their progress. Clarity in these areas has a positive effect on the work of collaborative teams (Ebrahim et al., 2009).

One of the most important steps members of virtual teams can take to build trust is to clarify their expectations by articulating the specific commitments they will make to one another to support their collective efforts. Establishing these unambiguous commitments is a critical step in determining whether members operate as a true team or merely as a loose collection of people who occasionally work together (Goleman, Boyatzis, & McKee, 2004). As Katzenbach and Smith (1993) write:

> At the heart of such long and, at times, difficult interactions lies a commitment-building process in which the whole team candidly explores who is best suited to each task. . . . In effect, it establishes a social contract among members that relates to their purpose, and guides and obligates how they must work together. . . . At its core, team accountability is about the sincere promises we make to ourselves and others, promises that underpin two critical aspects of teams: commitment and trust. (pp. 59–60)

Collectively creating this well-defined social contract, specifying the commitments members make to each other, is one of the most powerful strategies for building trust among members of virtual teams (Kirkman et al., 2002).

One way to approach establishing these team commitments or norms is to have members list the qualities and conditions they feel would contribute to an ideal team. The goal here is to identify specific, observable behaviors rather than esoteric beliefs. "We will recognize the spark of divinity that flows from the soul of each of our children" may sound morally impeccable, but it doesn't establish what members will actually *do* in the team process. Examples of effective collective commitments might include the following.

To promote the success of our team, I promise that I will:

- Be a positive, fully contributing member of our team

- Work to arrive at a consensus with my colleagues

- Honor the decisions made by my team

- Complete the work I am assigned on a timely basis

- Respond to questions from my teammates within twenty-four hours

- Stay fully engaged throughout all our meetings

- Share both my instructional practices and the evidence of student learning I gather

- Express my concerns and solicit feedback when I feel members are not honoring our commitments

Daniel Goleman and colleagues (2004) recommend that teams begin and end their meetings with a review of their collective commitments until those commitments become completely internalized. Establishing these commitments is not a perfunctory exercise to complete before getting to the real teamwork. It is an important step in increasing the likelihood of a positive experience for members and the ultimate success of the team. Failure to clarify expectations is one of the most common causes of team failure (Blanchard, 2007). Don't skip this important step on your virtual team journey!

Attention to Social Needs

The lack of social interaction is consistently cited as an issue on virtual teams (Kirkman et al., 2002). Lacking this interaction, members can feel isolated and detached rather than welcomed and significant as contributors to a collective, collegial effort. To address this challenge, organizers of virtual teams might consider the following strategies.

- **Bring team members together physically early in the process when possible.** Face-to-face communication is still better than virtual when it comes to building relationships. If geographic proximity allows, bring the team together, and use the time to help members get to know each other personally as well as professionally. Use both face-to-face and virtual meetings if possible (Watkins, 2013).

- **Simulate face-to-face interaction.** The best virtual teams do more than exchange emails and attachments. They use online chats and video conferencing to bring members together in ways that simulate on-site meetings (RW³ CultureWizard, 2010). A face-to-face meeting using a video-conferencing platform, such as Skype or GoToMeeting, can be more intimate than a meeting of ten people in the same room.

- **Create a "virtual watercooler."** As previously cited, the informal interactions that occur in the faculty dining room or department office are important elements in establishing relational bonds. Inattention to replicating these informal interactions can result in virtual team meetings that are so task focused that team cohesion is sacrificed. Therefore, virtual teams should take a few minutes at the beginning of a meeting to check in on each other—to discuss what is going well, challenges they are facing, and how they are feeling about the virtual team process. Occasional team-building exercises also can be used to inject some fun into meetings (Watkins, 2013).

- **Use social networking.** Many virtual teams find that social-networking tools not only help them stay connected with their colleagues but also enhance their personal relationships.

- **Maintain contact in between team meetings.** Team leaders should reach out to members on a consistent basis in ways that are not directly related to tasks. They should check in with members to determine how things are going and express appreciation for each individual's contribution to the collective effort. Leaders also should survey members periodically to solicit their assessments of how the team is doing and their ideas for improving it.

- **Distribute leadership.** When team leaders distribute leadership opportunities throughout a team, they help increase each member's engagement with and commitment to the team process (Watkins, 2013). Different members can take responsibility for leading a special project, facilitating team dialogue, mentoring a new team member, or sharing instructional strategies based on superior results on a common assessment.

Conclusion

PLCs represent an important bridge in taking educators from the assumptions and practices of the past to the more collaborative cultures of the present. Furthermore, PLCs are perfectly positioned to take the profession thoughtfully into the future. Educators can move from a model characterized by isolated teachers in isolated classrooms to a new reality wherein the ability to access teacher expertise throughout the world is available to every teacher and team. Combining the PLC process with the power of technology creates the potential to bring the profession together in the name of learning.

Our enthusiasm for the combined potential of PLCs and virtual collaboration to have a dramatic impact on student and adult learning is genuine. We also recognize, however, that neither creating time for educators to collaborate nor providing them with access to technology guarantees schools will become more effective. The challenge confronting educators is merging these powerful ideas in ways that help redefine the structure and culture of schooling.

We do not call attention to the challenges of implementing school-based PLCs and virtual collaboration to discourage educators from engaging in this important work. The task is difficult but doable. It should be approached with both a sense of realism and optimism. In the following chapters, we hope to provide educators and leaders with the tools they need to respond effectively to these challenges.

CHAPTER 2

Focusing on the Right Work

Although we are excited about the possibility of virtual collaborative teams having a major impact on schooling, we must also caution that if every teacher in America joins such a team, no gains will be made in either adult or student learning *unless members focus on the right work*. Collaboration is morally neutral. In a toxic culture, giving people time to collaborate simply reinforces the negative aspects of the culture. Without discipline, focus, and purpose, the collaborative spaces created by a virtual team can become an embarrassing platform for frivolous "coblabberation," a waste of time, and a missed opportunity rather than a catalyst for learning. Therefore, the more relevant question that members of virtual teams must keep in the forefront of their work is not, Are we collaborating? but rather, What are we collaborating *about*?

If educators are to engage in virtual collaboration that strengthens their capacity to create powerful PLCs—and help more students learn at higher levels than ever before—they must be clear on the meaning and implications of the term *professional learning community*. In every aspect of the PLC process, clarity precedes competence. Ambiguity regarding the purpose and practices of virtual collaboration diminishes the likelihood of having a positive impact on student and adult learning.

In chapter 1, we defined a PLC as an ongoing process in which educators work collaboratively in recurring cycles of collective inquiry and action research in order to achieve better results for the students they serve. We also stressed that the process rests on a solid foundation that can only be established through sustained, two-way dialogue that helps members to clarify:

- The purpose of their school or district (shared mission)

- The school they must create to achieve that purpose (shared vision)

- The collective commitments members must make in order to create such a school (shared values)

- The targets and time lines they must pursue to demonstrate progress in creating the school that achieves their collective purpose (shared goals)

Those engaging in virtual collaboration should consider slight modifications of these same questions.

- What is the purpose of our virtual collaboration?

- What is our vision of highly effective virtual collaboration? What specific processes must we put in place to achieve that vision?

- What commitments must we make to each other in order to foster the powerful virtual collaboration we envision?

- What targets and time lines must we establish to mark our progress and monitor the effectiveness of our virtual collaboration?

The Big Ideas

Three big ideas drive the dialogue that establishes the foundation of a PLC and, ultimately, give direction to every team member—whether communication is face to face or virtual. These big ideas are described in the following section.

1. Ensure that all students learn at high levels.

2. Work collaboratively to meet students' needs.

3. Create a results-oriented culture.

Ensure That All Students Learn at High Levels

The first big idea to drive the PLC process is that the fundamental purpose of school is to ensure all students learn at high levels. To ensure this big idea comes to life, members of virtual collaborative teams must address the following four critical questions for each unit they teach.

1. **What is it we want our students to know and be able to do?** What essential knowledge, skills, and dispositions must all students acquire as a result of this grade level, this course, and this unit we are about to teach? Can we agree there are certain skills and concepts all students must learn, regardless of which member of our team is teaching these students? What systems have we put in place to ensure we are providing every student with access to a guaranteed and viable curriculum?

2. **How will we know if our students are learning?** How can we check for understanding on an ongoing basis in our individual classrooms? How will we gather evidence of each student's learning as a team? What criteria will we establish to assess the quality of student work? How can we be certain we are able to apply the criteria consistently?

3. **How will we respond when students do not learn?** What steps can we establish to provide students who struggle with additional time and support for learning

in a way that is timely, directive, and systematic rather than invitational and random? How can we provide students with multiple opportunities to demonstrate their learning?

4. **How will we enrich and extend the learning for students who are proficient?** How can we differentiate instruction among us so that the needs of *all* students are met without relying on rigid tracking (DuFour, DuFour, Eaker, & Many, 2010)?

Work Collaboratively to Meet Students' Needs

The second big idea to drive the PLC process is that in order to help all students learn, educators must work collaboratively in a collective effort to meet the needs of each student. To ensure this idea comes to life, members of a virtual collaborative team must do the following.

- Work interdependently to achieve shared goals for which they are mutually accountable

- Embed time for collaboration into their routine practices

- Establish clarity on the purpose and priorities of their collaboration and stay focused on the right work

- Establish and honor commitments regarding how they work together

Create a Results-Oriented Culture

The third big idea to drive the PLC process is that in order to know if students are learning and respond appropriately to their needs, educators must create a results-oriented culture. They must be hungry for evidence of student learning and use that evidence to drive continuous improvement of the PLC process. To bring this big idea to life, members of a virtual collaborative team must ensure the following.

- Members work collaboratively with others on the team to achieve SMART goals that are:
    - Strategically and specifically aligned with school and district goals
    - Measurable
    - Attainable
    - Results oriented—that is, require evidence of higher levels of student learning for achievement
    - Time bound (Conzemius & O'Neill, 2014)

- Members work collaboratively with others on the team to gather and analyze evidence of student learning on a regular basis to inform and improve their professional practice as well as the collective practice of the team. Team members explore questions such as, Who among us is getting excellent results teaching this skill? How can we learn from one another? What is the area in which our students are having the most difficulty? What must we learn as a team in order to better address that area of difficulty? Where can we turn to support our collective learning?

- Members use evidence of student learning on a regular basis to identify the specific needs of individual students. They move beyond using data to make general observations about student achievement. They create processes to use assessment results to respond to students by name and by need.

- Members are willing to assess the effectiveness of every policy, program, procedure, and practice on the basis of its impact on student learning.

Conclusion

We anticipate that many busy educators will be tempted to rush through or entirely skip the foundational dialogue of virtual teams addressed in this chapter. They will want to get to the "real work" and begin discussions on a unit or skill they plan to teach. Resist this temptation! *Go slow to go fast.* Clarify the purpose of your virtual collaboration, describe how an ideal virtual team should operate, consider the commitments you are willing to make to your colleagues to create this ideal, and establish SMART goals that you will work together to achieve. Share your hopes and dreams, and strive to build consensus. With this solid foundation in place, you can begin your collective work with the clarity of purpose and focus that it demands.

CHAPTER 3

Organizing Virtual Connections

As we have emphasized, technology now makes it possible for educators to communicate and collaborate without regard to space and time and expand their perspectives beyond their unique situations. The benefits of access to different perspectives became evident to Casey in 2003 during the fifteen weeks he was teaching an online leadership course to a diverse group of educators. His students included Gretchen, an up-and-coming teacher leader in Chicago with a background in community service and a passionate commitment to leading substantive change in her city. She offered an urban perspective and was attempting to have a positive impact in one of the largest school districts in the United States.

Gina was employed as both a principal and a third-grade teacher in a very small rural school in North Dakota. The fact that her daughter was a student in her third-grade classroom meant she had the unique perspective of a principal, teacher, and mother all rolled into one.

Abe was from Minnesota but wasn't in the United States at the time of the class. Instead, he was stationed at a military facility in Iraq. By night, Abe led his troop of dedicated soldiers into battle in a life-or-death struggle in the Middle East. By day, he reflected in virtual collaborative learning spaces with his colleagues Gretchen, Gina, and other educators on the various leadership issues and theories presented in the class.

Although Gretchen, Gina, and Abe were applying their learning in very different situations, they were united by the fact that technology allowed them to create a small learning community to help them work through their respective challenges. The result was a dynamic learning experience wherein the hopes and aspirations of an energetic leader in a large urban district, the thoughtful diligence of the rural principal/teacher/mother, and the introspection of a courageous helicopter pilot leading his troops into battle provided the entire class with insights into the complexity of leadership that enriched their individual learning. As Marcel Proust (n.d.) wisely observed, "The real voyage of discovery consists not in seeking new landscapes, but in seeing with new eyes." The virtual community created by this online class gave each member access to "new eyes," fresh perspectives, and diverse thinking that proved extremely valuable to participants.

The ability to create virtual teams capable of benefiting from this rich cross section of human experience is now available to educators throughout the world. Collaborative teams can expand their memberships beyond the walls of their schools. They can have access to the advantages that accrue from seeing with new eyes.

The Imprecision of Virtual Teaming

The story of Gretchen, Gina, and Abe illustrates how virtual teaming connections can be game changing, allowing people from around the globe to collaborate. However, it is evident that, in many cases, educators are not using the power that advanced technology and connectivity make available to them. In fact, in many cases, they have been imprecise in how they use these spaces, and that imprecision can lead to confusion and missteps.

Several years ago, Casey was working with a medium-sized school district in Northern California. This district was experiencing declining student achievement, so it embraced the PLC model and was working through the inevitable implementation challenges. One of those challenges of interest to district leaders was the issue of getting creative with their teaming structures.

Kate was the enthusiastic assistant superintendent for instructional services in this district, and she was determined to use technology to enhance the creative capacity of her teachers and principals. She had spent her entire career in this middle-class community. As a result, she understood the culture shock her teachers were experiencing. Suddenly, the student demographics had shifted, and a large percentage of non-English-speaking students were coming to school each day. Kate explained that, for the most part, the adults were accepting of this shift, but they were largely unprepared for both the academic and social adjustments required to meet the needs of these students.

To address the challenge of serving this burgeoning population of English learners (ELs), Kate decided to create an opportunity for online dialogue about this issue. She thought that by using the available technology, she would be opening the door for a much broader and deeper conversation. She hoped that by involving more educators from throughout the district, she would encourage some of the younger teachers to chime in—assuming that digital natives would be more prone to express themselves online.

Virtual Teaming: Kate's Scenario

Kate launched the dialogue by writing a blog entry and sending an email to the entire staff under the subject line "Understanding Our English Learners." The email included a link to her blog and an invitation to the staff to contribute to the dialogue about serving ELs. Upon logging in, teachers found that Kate had posted a well-written blog entry that discussed the specific changes that had taken place over the years in terms of demographics and that described some of the current challenges that were particularly problematic. She also included links to several articles and a few videos on the topic of best practice approaches to serving ELs. She then invited all the district's approximately four hundred teachers to respond to the blog with ideas for improving services for this special group of students.

At first, Kate was very excited by the response. Teachers of ELs from several different levels shared observations and suggestions about what was happening to the ELs in their subject area. They specifically addressed some of the language barriers this particular group was experiencing and how their department or grade level teams had been addressing them. She was pleased to see the PLC at Work concept of vertical teaming in action. She also noted that several foreign language teachers and some social studies teachers had also joined the conversation by the end of day four.

By the end of the week, more surprises came. Kate noticed that several teachers from a neighboring district had joined the conversation. Apparently, one of her teachers had shared the link and password. Two members from the state department had somehow also been invited to participate. Kate then learned some foreign language teachers and English language arts teachers at the middle school had recently held a face-to-face meeting on the topic. Those teachers were bringing up decisions the department had made and were causing some confusion among other participants. Several teachers had logged on in an attempt to participate and concluded, with clear frustration, that they had somehow been omitted from earlier exchanges and were lacking much-needed information. Adding to this confusion, Kate started to get emails from some of her veteran teacher-friends who told her that there was a rumor that this threaded discussion was all a precursor to a new policy the board was secretly considering.

On Saturday at about noon, Kate got online to craft a message explaining to participants that no such policy change for ELs was looming. When she logged on, she noticed an angry virtual threaded exchange had occurred between a high school art teacher and an elementary school reading specialist. Someone made an accusation of racism, which generated a series of angry responses delivered in ALL CAPS to make sure each recipient would notice the message.

To make matters worse, the state department representative had shared her disappointment in the crassness of the discussion. Kate began to wonder if this dialogue was subject to the Freedom of Information Act regulations and, thus, could end up in the evening newspaper. She picked up her cell phone and contacted her technology coordinator to beg him to take down the threaded conversation before more damage was done.

What Did Kate Do Wrong?

Before we reflect on Kate's situation, let's consider some of the strengths in her approach. First, her district had embraced the PLC process. Educators were used to working together to solve problems, so she went into the virtual collaboration experience knowing that her colleagues understood the power of collaboration, the norms associated with good dialogue within a team, and the merits of developing new levels of shared knowledge. She also listed some good sources and offered cogent thoughts to hopefully shape the discussion. She used a learning modality well suited for thoughtful dialogue and team learning. Finally, Kate was a respected leader whose many years of positive interactions in the district gave her considerable credibility with teachers.

Yet, despite her good intentions, Kate made the mistake of assuming that human beings automatically transpose the habits of communication in face-to-face conversations into virtual learning spaces. She quickly learned that her assumption was incorrect, particularly with teachers who have spent little time communicating and collaborating, even casually, in cyberspace.

Initially, Kate failed to engineer the appropriate e-connection. She didn't establish clear parameters for membership. She positioned the conversation to theoretically take place among four hundred educators. While there may be circumstances in which it is appropriate to engineer an e-connection to even larger groups of educators, this number was too large to facilitate the high levels of thoughtful interconnectivity, discussion, and collaboration she sought. She didn't clearly define the goals of the interaction or future action items that might result from the discussion. Even though teachers were used to working together and each team had established its own set of collective commitments, Kate didn't take the time to establish that this virtual collaboration also should be commitment driven. She failed to establish any other specific guidelines or expectations for interaction in virtual learning spaces. Given the uniqueness of learning and collaborating at a distance, specific protocols for e-collaboration also must be established in order to promote meaningful collaboration.

Implementing Virtual Teaming

In the chapters that follow, we discuss the three strategic levels for implementing virtual teaming in a PLC. We provide a brief overview here of the three levels and then use the rest of this chapter to illustrate the specific protocols for Level 1. Figure 3.1 illustrates these three levels.

Level 1	Level 2	Level 3
Engineering a Strategic e-Connection	**Strategizing for e-Collaboration**	**Enhancing Learning With e-Acceleration**
• Choosing the right type of virtual collaborative opportunity	• Utilizing best practices for basic online communication and collaboration	• Using asynchronous communication and open-source strategies to accelerate learning

Figure 3.1: Virtual teaming in a PLC.

Level 1: Engineering a Strategic e-Connection

Before exploring Level 1, Engineering a Strategic e-Connection, keep in mind that these strategies should be implemented in conjunction with establishing other elements essential to effective teaming in a PLC. When creating norms, we recommend that those norms be observed when teachers collaborate in virtual and face-to-face learning spaces. Furthermore, observing collective commitments and ongoing development of shared knowledge should be enhanced by the execution of strategies we explore. Honoring these strategies increases the likelihood of quality outcomes.

In order to maximize the capacity of virtual teaming, educators should engineer their collaborative e-learning spaces to avoid distraction and maximize the opportunity for growth. We offer a model with ten working dimensions that allows educators to pick and choose (and engineer) the best strategic collaborative structure available, given the learning objective at hand. Each dimension within this structure changes the interaction and provides opportunities and pathways for growth. Had Kate utilized this model, she likely would have organized her work much differently.

Level 2: Strategizing for e-Collaboration

Have you ever sent a text message or instant message (IM) and been misunderstood? Have you ever received an email from someone wherein the message was rather benign but the feeling or tone of the message seemed cold or angry? Casey's mother, a retired principal, types messages in all caps on Facebook. Luckily, she's so well liked that recipients are willing to overlook that she appears to be SHOUTING.

Level 2 provides specific strategies to help team members improve the communication process, avoid derailing disconnects, and enhance the opportunity to create a learning space that is dynamic and authentic.

Level 3: Enhancing Learning With e-Acceleration

Finally, Level 3 strategies are designed to accelerate learning beyond previously experienced levels. The basic assumption here is that collaborating at a distance isn't just a convenient and efficient alternative to meeting face to face. When done well, virtual teaming can significantly improve the quality, depth, and applicability of the learning made possible in face-to-face teams in a PLC. We describe the process of open sourcing to address school challenges and use the wisdom and experience of "the crowd" to provide new levels of feedback to local teams working within PLC schools and districts.

The power of the crowd references the almost limitless capacity technology can bring to a challenge or problem-solving endeavor. The notion of using the crowd is based on the assumption that when outside voices are allowed to participate openly in a conversation or contribute to an opportunity to innovate, the crowd itself begins to sort out the best ideas and allows them to bubble up to the surface. The better ideas, for example, receive more virtual attention and, through collaboration and reflection, may ultimately be improved. Fewer innovative solutions are then left hanging in virtual abeyance, unsupported by the crowd (Howe, 2009). This emerging idea continues to require thoughtful experimentation. Our hope is that the emergence of these outside innovative voices will accelerate the work of PLC teams and allow them to innovate at ever-increasing levels of effectiveness.

We also illustrate the power of *asynchronous* discussions. When you go to a conference, you must arrive at a time that's synchronized with the speaker's starting and ending times. When you stand face to face with somebody and listen to a lecture or collaborate on a group project, the time and experience are synchronized. A third-grade teacher doing a live demonstration for her students is using synchronous learning—learning that is happening in real time. A collaborative team meeting at a designated place and time within a school is yet another example of synchronous learning. It is important to keep in mind, however, that synchronous forms of collaboration don't necessarily have to be face-to-face, flesh-and-bone experiences. A designated time for weekly teacher meetings in different schools using Skype to connect is an example of a virtual synchronous learning experience. In this instance, educators simply use the power of technology to meet with one another where geography is a barrier.

Asynchronous learning removes the barriers of both time and space (Bonk, 2009; Tu & Corry, 2003). Accessing the Khan Academy on your home computer with your child to review concepts or access homework online represents an asynchronous learning opportunity. You don't have to be synchronized with the teacher's schedule or the proverbial bell; and if you need extra time to think something through, you can have it. Posting a thought or idea on a blog, and having multiple participants reflect on the content and debate with one another, is another example of an asynchronous learning dynamic. Communication opportunities aren't bound by planning periods. Participants can jump in and add value whenever it's convenient for them. Asynchronous learning allows team members to participate at times when perhaps their energy levels are higher or when the kids are finally asleep, which allows for levels of concentration necessary to bring forth the best they have to offer. Done well and with strategic intent, asynchronous learning spaces can promote deep levels of input from others and provide team members with generous amounts of "think time" to digest and synthesize the learning.

Ten Dimensions for Engineering a Strategic e-Connection

Many strategic decisions go into engineering a quality learning space for virtual teams. The degree to which organizers are thoughtful in making these decisions significantly impacts the quality of the work. The ten dimensions of the decisions impacting virtual collaborative teams are illustrated in figure 3.2 (page 52).

1. Membership • Open • Closed	2. Connection • Virtual • Face to face • Hybrid
3. Scope • Team • School • Local district • Regional/state • National/international	4. Format • Asynchronous (virtual) • Synchronous (face to face or virtual) • Hybrid

5. Orientation
 	
• Grade level / content area
 	
• Function
   a. Exploratory
   b. School improvement
   c. Looking for examples
	6. Duration
	
	• Ongoing
	
	• Term (short, long, midrange, and so on)

7. Origin • Planned • Unplanned	8. Purpose • Ignite/inform • Learn and transform • Give voice / send a message
9. Size • Limited • Unlimited	10. Management • Direct • Facilitative • Minimal

Figure 3.2: Ten dimensions for engineering a strategic e-connection.

1. Membership: Open or Closed

Best for closed membership (handwritten annotation)

The dimension of membership refers to individuals who are selected or invited to participate in a virtual learning space. In this context, there are two choices with membership—open or closed.

If a membership is closed, it represents a learning space that is strategically engineered only to be available to a select group of participants. Collaborative teams within a PLC are, by their nature, closed groups. If these teams utilize virtual teaming and technology to enhance their work, they would represent a closed virtual team.

An e-connection space engineered to be open is, by definition, available to a much larger (or potentially unlimited) group of participants. An open virtual group with an unlimited number of members coming and going would not provide the level of connection and interdependence needed to function as a true collaborative *team*—a group of people working interdependently to achieve shared goals for which members are mutually accountable. There are, however, occasions in which engineering opportunities for connecting with open levels of participation offer a unique opportunity for learning and innovation. Chapter 5 of this book is devoted to the concept of open sourcing, wherein we describe growth and innovation opportunities teams can experience when they reach beyond their school or district boundaries and pursue the power and potential that are available with the creative forces on the web.

A modified version of open membership might include extending an invitation to a more defined population. For example, if members of a middle school mathematics team are interested in having an open discussion regarding teaching a particular concept in their subject area, they could contact the National Council of Teachers of Mathematics (NCTM) and invite midlevel mathematics educators from within that large professional organization to participate. In this case, the team would not control exactly who joined the conversation, but it could at least steer the conversation toward participants with common interests and content expertise.

The decision to utilize an open or closed format has a significant impact on the way a team works and its members' opportunities to interact, learn, and grow. Educators who are committed to working as members of a virtual collaborative team (that is, working interdependently to achieve shared goals for which members are mutually accountable) usually opt for a closed structure. However, they can always choose to pose questions or issues in an open forum. Figure 3.3 further describes the dimension of membership.

Membership: Kate's Scenario

In the previous scenario, Kate engineered the e-collaboration regarding ELs to be totally open. This probably was not the best strategy because she was actually seeking a more thoughtful, intimate discussion about this sensitive topic. In this case, Kate might have been better off establishing a closed structure while choosing teachers from across the district, potentially representing a variety of grade levels and disciplines. A closed approach, including about fifteen participants, could have created a collaborative and problem-solving dynamic that was more manageable, wherein Kate could more directly interact with participants, ask for clarification, and dig for deeper meaning behind some of the thoughts expressed.

2. Connection: Virtual, Face to Face, or Hybrid

Connections can be virtual, face to face, or a hybrid of the two. The traditional meeting context for most school-based collaborative teams in PLCs is face to face. A 100 percent virtual connection means that the group does not meet face to face due to geographic restrictions or challenges in synchronizing calendars. For example, many schools have established teams of singleton teachers who may need to collaborate with other teachers from a large geographic area. If this type of group never meets face to face but instead, uses a shared web space for ongoing levels of interaction, it would represent a 100 percent virtual team.

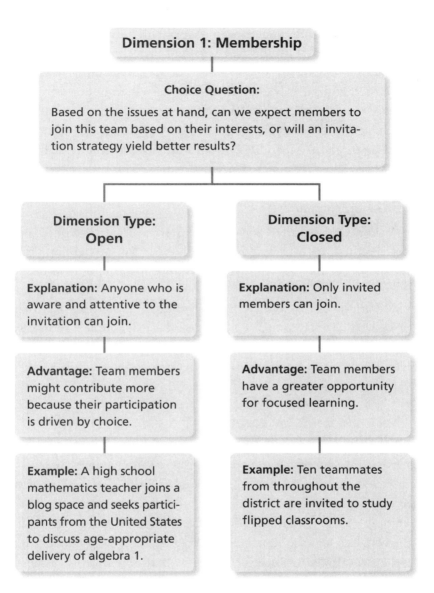

Dimension 1: Membership

Choice Question:

Based on the issues at hand, can we expect members to join this team based on their interests, or will an invitation strategy yield better results?

Dimension Type: Open

Explanation: Anyone who is aware and attentive to the invitation can join.

Advantage: Team members might contribute more because their participation is driven by choice.

Example: A high school mathematics teacher joins a blog space and seeks participants from the United States to discuss age-appropriate delivery of algebra 1.

Dimension Type: Closed

Explanation: Only invited members can join.

Advantage: Team members have a greater opportunity for focused learning.

Example: Ten teammates from throughout the district are invited to study flipped classrooms.

Figure 3.3: Dimension 1—membership.

A hybrid connection takes advantage of both face-to-face and virtual connections. With this type of connection, the learning space is engineered to allow for ongoing face-to-face interaction supported by virtual collaborative opportunities. A well-engineered hybrid collaborative learning space doesn't just use the e-connection as a convenient tool for keeping notes and staying organized. Facilitators actually extend the learning by continuing conversations that may have started in a face-to-face meeting with technology-driven learning threads or virtual spaces designed to solicit information from beyond the team meeting.

A hybrid connection is arguably the most fertile in terms of opportunities for teams to strengthen their knowledge and develop their capacities. Well-run, face-to-face meetings with ongoing levels of virtual connection allow a greater sense of continuity in pursuit of new learning objectives to enhance and expand the team's learning process. In chapters 4 and 5, we explore Level 2 and Level 3 of this model by presenting specific steps to enhance the connections and learning in traditional, face-to-face team meetings within a PLC. Figure 3.4 further describes the dimension of connection.

Connection: Kate's Scenario

Kate engineered an entirely virtual collaboration. However, because participants were from the same district, the opportunity for face-to-face dialogue regarding ELs was highly likely. Membership was open, so there was no way of telling the degree to which teachers knew one another or might communicate virtually while continuing the conversation over lunch with colleagues. While there is nothing wrong with that, engineering the collaboration with this in mind allows for more thoughtful connections. In keeping with the earlier suggestion of identifying a small task force to study the issue, committing the team to several face-to-face meetings, along with an extended opportunity to dialogue in an asynchronous virtual space, could create more meaningful discussions both online and in person. By definition, this would be a hybrid approach.

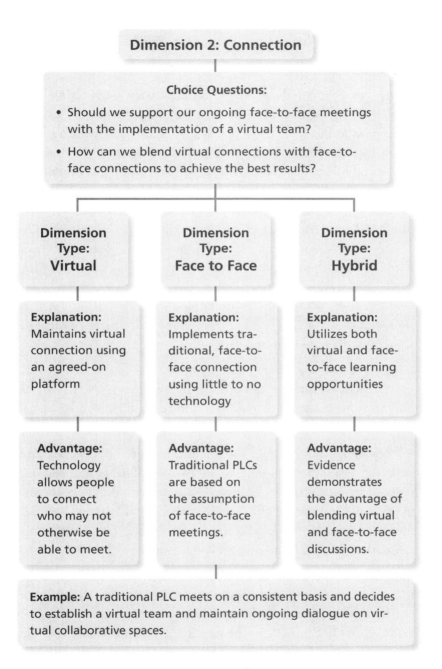

Dimension 2: Connection

Choice Questions:

- Should we support our ongoing face-to-face meetings with the implementation of a virtual team?
- How can we blend virtual connections with face-to-face connections to achieve the best results?

Dimension Type: **Virtual**	Dimension Type: **Face to Face**	Dimension Type: **Hybrid**
Explanation: Maintains virtual connection using an agreed-on platform	**Explanation:** Implements traditional, face-to-face connection using little to no technology	**Explanation:** Utilizes both virtual and face-to-face learning opportunities
Advantage: Technology allows people to connect who may not otherwise be able to meet.	**Advantage:** Traditional PLCs are based on the assumption of face-to-face meetings.	**Advantage:** Evidence demonstrates the advantage of blending virtual and face-to-face discussions.

Example: A traditional PLC meets on a consistent basis and decides to establish a virtual team and maintain ongoing dialogue on virtual collaborative spaces.

Figure 3.4: Dimension 2—connection.

3. Scope: Team, School, Local District, Regional/State, or National/International

The scope of virtual collaboration refers to the engineering decision team organizers must make regarding the parameters of a team's strategic e-connection. The scope of collaborative teams in a school using the PLC process would typically include grade-level teams, course- or subject matter-specific teams, vertical teams, or interdisciplinary teams—all of which meet on a consistent basis. The scope of their work in this case would be characterized by the *right work* of the PLC process, which includes working as a collaborative team to accomplish shared goals, establishing a guaranteed and viable curriculum, gathering evidence of student learning on an ongoing basis through team-developed common formative assessments, using assessment results to identify strengths and weaknesses in instruction, and creating systematic interventions that provide struggling students with extra time and support.

School-based teams also could be open to others in the district. For example, we know of districts in which singleton teachers in one building join a collaborative team in another, utilizing both face-to-face and virtual teaming to facilitate the work.

The scope of a team could also include members from throughout a specific region or state, or it could include national or international representation. In these instances, the collaboration likely is more manageable and meaningful if the membership is limited to a small number of representatives who commit to working interdependently rather than to all the potentially eligible teachers.

Perhaps the best way to illustrate scope would be to think about it in terms of a more contemporary application. Let's assume that our friend Kate from Northern California noticed that the mathematics scores in her district were steadily declining on both state and locally created assessments. To address this issue and study potential solutions, grade-level and content-area teams in the schools certainly could analyze the problem and attempt to identify solutions. The scope of the work is team based.

If, in tackling this problem, Kate decided she wanted to look beyond the school or district level, she could work with teacher leaders from her district and attempt to assemble teams that included other mathematics educators from throughout her region or state. Once again, if she was expecting deep levels of interaction, she could try to limit the size of this group and create a small but focused group of mathematics educators dealing with similar issues in student achievement. She also could consider team membership beyond the state by connecting with national collaborative spaces. The NEA Professional Practice Communities provides facilitated collaborative spaces for mathematics educators at all levels from throughout the nation. These asynchronous national learning spaces are facilitated by assigned mathematics educators and provide a venue for people like Kate and her colleagues to engineer a team with a national and potentially international scope. Keep in mind that with each choice comes an opportunity to expand growth and potentially challenge local presuppositions and assumptions while also presenting greater logistical and engineering challenges.

Finally, scope is not dependent on the size of the team. A large high school may have twenty teachers who teach the same course and are, therefore, a team, while a statewide initiative to support and strengthen PLCs could limit membership to ten representatives. Scope refers primarily to the degree to which membership is local or beyond, and the decision regarding scope depends on what is to be accomplished. Figure 3.5 (pages 60–61) further describes the dimension of scope.

Scope: Kate's Scenario

Kate was clearly looking for input beyond the team and school levels. Based on her response, she was not prepared for a regional, state, national, or international discussion to unfold. Kate had intended to engineer an e-connection limited to the local district. Given the depth

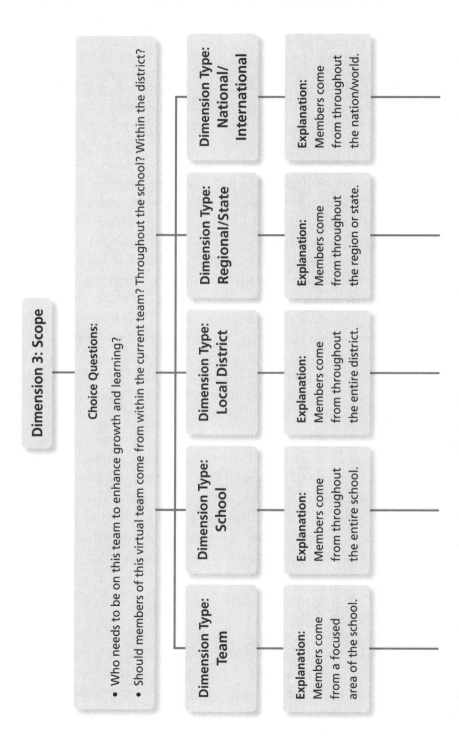

Dimension 3: Scope

Choice Questions:

- Who needs to be on this team to enhance growth and learning?
- Should members of this virtual team come from within the current team? Throughout the school? Within the district?

**Dimension Type:
Team**

Explanation:
Members come
from a focused
area of the school.

**Dimension Type:
School**

Explanation:
Members come
from throughout
the entire school.

**Dimension Type:
Local District**

Explanation:
Members come
from throughout
the entire district.

**Dimension Type:
Regional/State**

Explanation:
Members come
from throughout
the region or state.

**Dimension Type:
National/
International**

Explanation:
Members come
from throughout
the nation/world.

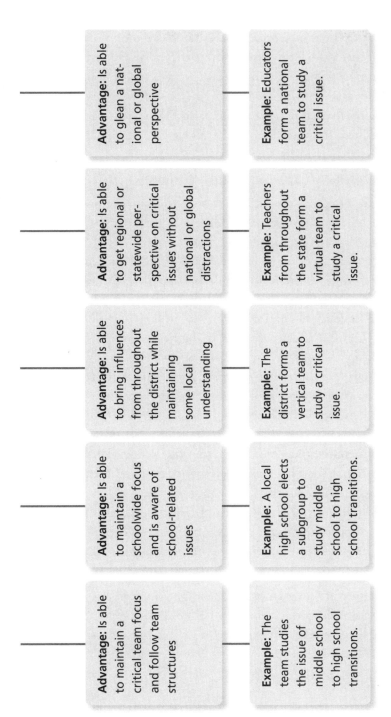

Advantage: Is able to maintain a critical team focus and follow team structures

Example: The team studies the issue of middle school to high school transitions.

Advantage: Is able to maintain a schoolwide focus and is aware of school-related issues

Example: A local high school elects a subgroup to study middle school to high school transitions.

Advantage: Is able to bring influences from throughout the district while maintaining some local understanding

Example: The district forms a vertical team to study a critical issue.

Advantage: Is able to get regional or statewide perspective on critical issues without national or global distractions

Example: Teachers from throughout the state form a virtual team to study a critical issue.

Advantage: Is able to glean a national or global perspective

Example: Educators form a national team to study a critical issue.

Figure 3.5: Dimension 3—scope.

and dimension of the topic at hand, this was a very good proposed approach. However, the lack of direction at inception created confusion. Certain participants interpreted the conversation as fodder for team-level discussions and decisions. Others saw it as a state-level conversation and invited outside participants. No one was wrong. Kate just failed to communicate her intentions.

4. Format: Asynchronous, Synchronous, or Hybrid

Previously, we discussed the difference between synchronous and asynchronous learning. Educators could elect to use either of these formats; however, in this area, we recommend the genius of "and" rather than the tyranny of "or" (Collins & Porras, 1997). For example, using the asynchronous format to simply post an idea or question, and then inviting others to comment at their leisure, is perfectly appropriate for a collegial relationship of like-minded people. This format is also useful if a team member is absent from the meeting or is "off track" in a year-round setting. These educators may not be physically present at the meeting. However, if the team uses a format that allows for easy access to information from the meeting as well as creates a forum to provide feedback and ask questions, the educators are more likely to feel like part of the team. If educators are to function as members of a true *team*, a specific time for collaboration should be embedded in their routine work practice. Members commit to one another that they will honor this "sacred" time and be present and prepared for team meetings. They should also, however, have the opportunity to post ideas, questions, reflections, and products for the consideration of their teammates at times that are convenient to members in between regularly scheduled meetings.

To further illustrate how an organizer might think about these choices, let's go back to the example of Kate. Posting a link and asking for feedback at the convenience of the recipient represents asynchronous levels of communication. If Kate organized a meeting using Skype, GoToMeeting, or a live web event, the e-connection would then be synchronous. If she decided to have a series of face-to-face meetings after school; some live events; and then some opportunities for focused, asynchronous posting and reflection, the connection would be a hybrid. Each decision obviously creates different levels of interaction and could potentially either enhance or detract from the learning opportunity.

Finally, asynchronous conversations don't have to be engineered to last forever. In fact, they are usually much more effective if recipients are given 24/7 access to them but are asked to provide their feedback within a specified amount of time. Generally speaking, the deeper the challenge or more perplexing the issue at hand, the more time you should provide for asynchronous conversations in order for the deepest thinking to emerge. In later chapters, we discuss how to facilitate these conversations to yield the best learning opportunities for all. Figure 3.6 (page 64) further describes the dimension of format.

Format: Kate's Scenario

In this case, Kate probably made the right decision in attempting to create an asynchronous, extended conversation about ELs. In many instances, our most thoughtful reflections regarding important educational topics are reduced to rushed synchronous comments lost in brief exchanges before and after meetings. Taking time to think about what you want to say, reflecting on a colleague's post, seeking out a source, or simply logging in when an idea strikes are all examples of advantageous asynchronous collaboration. If Kate had more thoughtfully prepared a focus group and asked members to meet perhaps at the beginning and the end of the process, by definition, the format would be a hybrid.

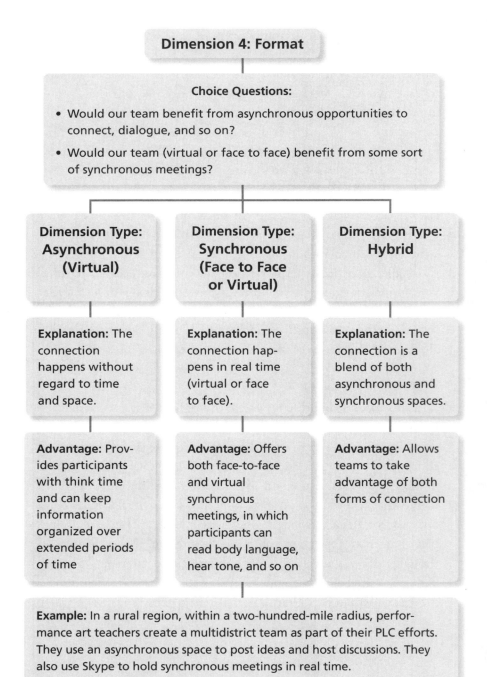

Dimension 4: Format

Choice Questions:

- Would our team benefit from asynchronous opportunities to connect, dialogue, and so on?
- Would our team (virtual or face to face) benefit from some sort of synchronous meetings?

Dimension Type: Asynchronous (Virtual)	Dimension Type: Synchronous (Face to Face or Virtual)	Dimension Type: Hybrid
Explanation: The connection happens without regard to time and space.	**Explanation:** The connection happens in real time (virtual or face to face).	**Explanation:** The connection is a blend of both asynchronous and synchronous spaces.
Advantage: Provides participants with think time and can keep information organized over extended periods of time	**Advantage:** Offers both face-to-face and virtual synchronous meetings, in which participants can read body language, hear tone, and so on	**Advantage:** Allows teams to take advantage of both forms of connection

Example: In a rural region, within a two-hundred-mile radius, performance art teachers create a multidistrict team as part of their PLC efforts. They use an asynchronous space to post ideas and host discussions. They also use Skype to hold synchronous meetings in real time.

Figure 3.6: Dimension 4—format.

5. Orientation: Grade Level / Content Area or Function

The most effective collaborative teams within school-based PLCs typically are organized by grade level or content area, and this format should serve as the basic structure of virtual teams as well. Schools also can benefit, however, when educators are organized into short-term task forces or long-term guiding coalitions. Task forces are ad-hoc groups called together for a defined period of time and charged with solving a problem or improving an organization. Adlai E. Stevenson High School in Lincolnshire, Illinois, has used task forces to become one of the most effective PLCs in the United States. Task forces have addressed topics such as creating a compelling vision of a school's future, using standards-based grading, developing effective systems of intervention, and expanding student participation in cross-curricular activities. Members are responsible for helping the entire staff build shared knowledge about an issue, proposing alternative solutions, and building consensus for action. These action-oriented "adhocracy" groups have been described as "*the* most powerful tools we have for effecting change" in organizations (Waterman, 1993, p. 16).

A guiding coalition represents a stabler leadership structure to monitor school improvement efforts. As a decade-long study of leadership by the Wallace Foundation (2012) concludes:

> A broad and longstanding consensus in leadership theory holds that leaders in all walks of life and all kinds of organizations, public and private, need to depend on others to accomplish the group's purpose and need to encourage the development of leadership across the organization. (p. 6)

Whereas John Kotter (1996) calls for a guiding coalition, Jim Collins (2001) refers to getting "the right people on the bus" (p. 13). Robert Marzano, Timothy Waters, and Brian McNulty (2005) discuss the imperative of a leadership team, and the message is consistent: the best organizations promote widely distributed leadership.

We will address the importance of dispersed leadership more fully in chapter 8.

Technology can assist in all three of these formats—team, task force, and guiding coalition. A grade-level team can link with other educators in that grade level to establish common essential outcomes, pacing, and assessments. Members can share results of common assessments to help inform and improve their practice. Task force members can use technology to research their issues and reach out to other educators around the world for ideas in addressing a problem. They can then use technology to provide every faculty member with access to resources and information. A guiding coalition can create a partnership with its school that is highly effective in improving student achievement. It can post dashboards to help faculty members track the progress of initiatives and monitor results. Figure 3.7 further describes the dimension of orientation.

Orientation: Kate's Scenario

Once again, Kate arguably made the right call from an engineering standpoint. Meeting the needs of ELs within an entire K–12 district is not a topic sequestered to a particular content area or grade level. It requires cross-curricular and multigrade-level perspectives.

6. Duration: Ongoing or Term

The PLC process is, by definition, a commitment to ongoing learning. Simply put, the work never ends. Those truly committed to continuous improvement recognize that their journey does not have a finish line. But as noted previously in our description of ad-hoc task forces, educators can also come together for defined periods of time for a specific purpose. For example, the mathematics, science, and technology teachers in a school may elect to work together to develop an integrated project that calls on students to apply learning from all three subject areas. A short-term team such as this can create a sense of energy and serve as a powerful catalyst for shared learning.

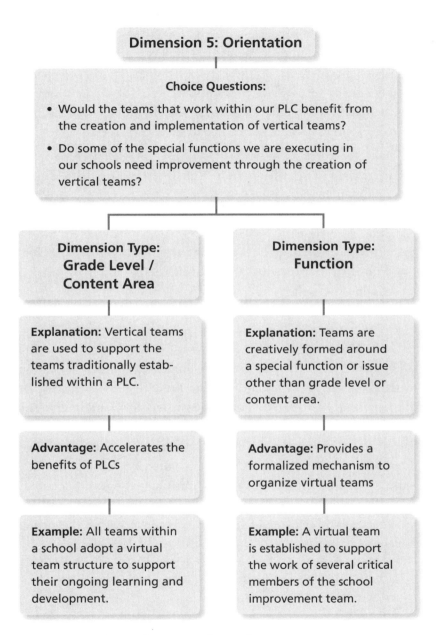

Figure 3.7: Dimension 5—orientation.

A virtual learning space engineered for an ongoing PLC collaborative team should provide team members with a place to share resources, present ideas, post reactions, maintain records, and engage in dialogue as a follow-up to team meetings. The virtual learning space should help to reinforce team reflection, problem solving, and learning so members are better able to achieve their goals.

Finally, even teams with a well-organized virtual learning space to support ongoing collaboration benefits from well-defined time lines for completing key events on the PLC journey. The best PLCs encourage action orientation and learning by *doing* rather than paralysis by analysis. Articulating targets and time lines for finishing critical work encourages ongoing teams to keep moving forward on their journey. Figure 3.8 further describes the dimension of duration.

Duration: Kate's Scenario

Kate clearly engineered this collaboration to have a beginning and an end. Thus, by definition, the duration of this collaboration would be term. However, by failing to make the timeframe clear at the beginning, the group flailed away without any kind of deadline in mind. In fact, some of the negative behavior that emerged might have resulted from a sense of fear or uncertainty about an imagined impending decision. By specifying at the onset the goals and intentions of the group as well as a specific timeframe for providing input, Kate likely would have de-escalated the conversation and provided participants with clear guidelines on how to interact in the virtual collaborative process. At some point, Kate could have created a group to study the topic over a longer period of time and continue to reflect on cross-curricular, multigrade-level, best practice approaches.

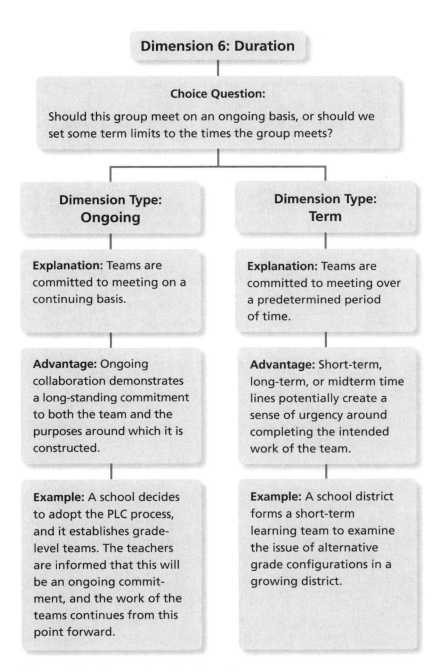

Dimension 6: Duration

Choice Question:

Should this group meet on an ongoing basis, or should we set some term limits to the times the group meets?

Dimension Type: Ongoing

Explanation: Teams are committed to meeting on a continuing basis.

Advantage: Ongoing collaboration demonstrates a long-standing commitment to both the team and the purposes around which it is constructed.

Example: A school decides to adopt the PLC process, and it establishes grade-level teams. The teachers are informed that this will be an ongoing commit-ment, and the work of the teams continues from this point forward.

Dimension Type: Term

Explanation: Teams are committed to meeting over a predetermined period of time.

Advantage: Short-term, long-term, or midterm time lines potentially create a sense of urgency around completing the intended work of the team.

Example: A school district forms a short-term learning team to examine the issue of alternative grade configurations in a growing district.

Figure 3.8: Dimension 6—duration.

7. Origin: Planned or Unplanned

Because the PLC process is ongoing, virtual collaborative teams should meet on a continuing basis according to an agreed-on plan. The plan not only should include when members should meet but also the purpose, tasks, goals, norms, and protocols to guide and inform their work.

While the notion of a team that develops organically sounds like the antithesis of a formally engineered team structure, it is important to recognize both the presence and legitimacy of organically developed teams formed to support spontaneous professional development or shared interests. A teacher in Kate's school, for example, may organically meet others in a professional collaborative space (such as the NEA Professional Practice Communities) and discover some sort of innovation germane to a challenge he or she is facing. This teacher may share the information with his or her team or link teammates to that outside connection. As educators learn to better connect with each other, these organic learning opportunities can offer a valuable structure and resource for tapping into the knowledge of others to solve local problems.

This notion of an unplanned, organic connection is already occurring. For example, many teachers of advanced placement (AP) courses have created organic groups based on their subject areas to share ideas on how to prepare students for success on AP exams. Many sites are designed to help teachers who face the challenge of implementing Common Core curriculum share their concerns and strategies. MasteryConnect offers a site where educators can create test item banks for different grade levels and subjects. The Teaching Channel provides educators with a place to pose questions, contribute to debates, observe videos of each other in the classroom, and solicit advice. Twitter sites, such as #SBLChat, #EdChat, and #SATChat, bring together international groups of teachers to address specific questions in real time.

Technology has given educators a chance to find each other, share what they know and believe, and expand their thinking in areas that are most relevant to them. Members of virtual collaborative teams should be open to the possibility that these groups can provide a pathway to innovation. We expand on this in chapter 5, where we talk about open sourcing. Figure 3.9 (page 72) further describes the dimension of origin.

Origin: Kate's Scenario

This was definitely a planned collaboration. However, Kate's lack of structure and engineering arguably gave it a rather unplanned feel. Had she invested in the other engineering elements discussed so far, this planned collaboration could have met its learning objectives.

8. Purpose: Ignite/Inform, Learn and Transform, or Give Voice / Send a Message

Effective PLCs ignite, inform, learn, and transform. They provide a framework for action research, deep learning, and continuous improvement. Therefore, a virtual learning space devoted to the purpose of igniting, informing, learning, and transforming basically would be utilizing technology and collaborative spaces to do the work of teams within PLCs.

A virtual learning space can, however, also exist to give voice and send a message. Almost everyone reading this book has undoubtedly seen learning platforms assembled to address issues or challenges. Those who oppose or endorse the Common Core, for example, may utilize a collaborative learning space to give voice to their concerns and invite others to react to their positions. These spaces can be controversial and degenerate into grouping by griping. Nonetheless, PLCs operate from the premise that when attempting to build consensus, all points of view (including dissent) not only should be heard but also should be solicited. Building shared knowledge is an essential aspect of the PLC process, and transparency is vital to

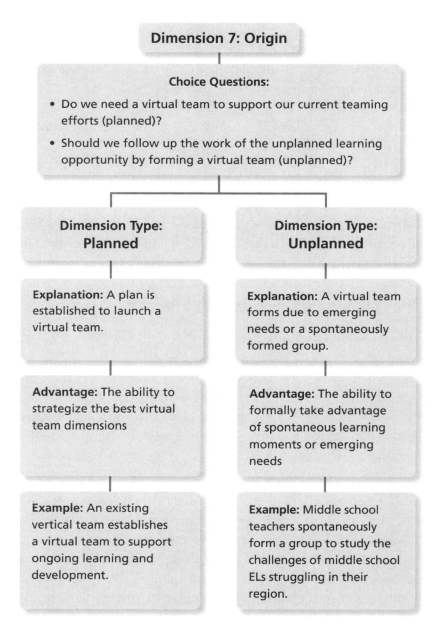

Figure 3.9: Dimension 7—origin.

building shared knowledge. Participants in a virtual learning space should be challenged to support their claims with research and evidence, but little is to be gained from censoring dissenting points of view. It is entirely appropriate, therefore, to use technology for allowing individual educators to voice their concerns about the trends and innovations impacting their work. Figure 3.10 (page 74) further describes the dimension of purpose.

Purpose: Kate's Scenario

To some degree, Kate made the mistake of trying to engineer an all-inclusive purpose. She knew that some of her colleagues lacked information about ELs, and she was hoping to inform them. She also was hoping for the learning and transformation that come from intimate, thoughtful, asynchronous discussions. Finally, Kate wanted to send a message that this topic wasn't going away anytime soon and it simply had to be addressed. However, participants became frustrated because they didn't know which purpose to pursue in the dialogue. The type of thoughtful debate and reflection needed to learn and transform requires the abilities to ask questions, propose all kinds of solutions, reflect, and experiment. If participants feel like this brainstorming synergy is a pathway to imminent, significant change, it's highly likely that emotions could take over and minimize the impact. In this case, Kate probably should have engineered this group to learn and transform, giving them opportunities to learn from one another, reflect on various ideas, and better conceptualize the issue before trying to solve what might be the chasm between where they are and where they want to be.

9. Size: Limited or Unlimited

Researchers have been unable to arrive at a consensus regarding the optimum size of a team, whether it is virtual or face to face. There have been powerful teams of two—the Wright Brothers, Lennon and McCartney, and Brin and Page (the creators of Google). Large teams have also accomplished great things. Steve Jobs created a team

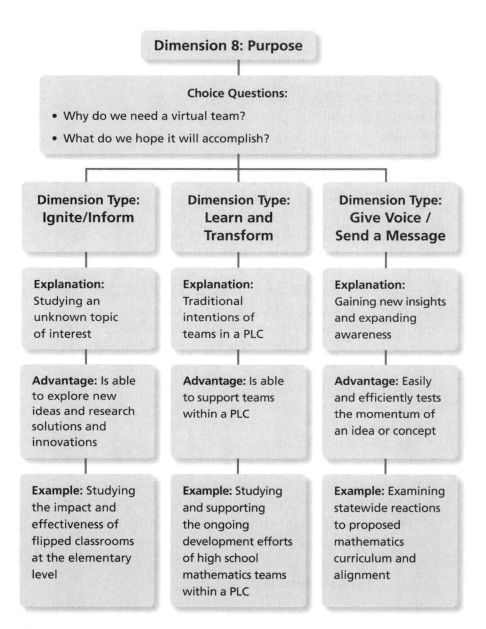

Figure 3.10: Dimension 8—purpose.

of fifty people to develop the Macintosh computer. The Manhattan Project, which oversaw the creation of the atomic bomb, was the largest collaboration of scientists in the history of the United States up to that time. More than 150,000 engineers, contractors, military personnel, and construction workers contributed to the project. In her book *Team Moon*, Catherine Thimmesh (2006) refers to the 400,000 people who worked on the *Apollo 11* project as the greatest team ever.

It would, therefore, be completely arbitrary to attempt to declare the definitive optimum size for the collaborative teams of either school-based or virtual PLCs. It also would be foolish for eight teachers assigned to teach sophomore English to exclude one member from participating on the team because they decided that seven was the optimum number.

The size of a team certainly impacts the way the team operates. A team of twenty-five members will function differently from one with four or five members. The larger team more likely will divide tasks among smaller subgroups, convene more frequently in subgroups, and reserve larger team meetings for reviewing recommendations and making decisions.

The goals of a virtual team are also a factor in determining team size. A team committed to helping the AP physics teachers in a district improve student achievement on AP exams will undoubtedly have fewer members than a national group of educators interested in exploring strategies for teaching the Common Core standards in language arts.

In general, establishing some limit on team size is necessary to foster the interaction, interdependence, shared goals, and mutual accountability characteristics of true teams. We recommend that the virtual team itself has the major voice in determining when the number of participants calls for division into subgroups or when membership should be closed because the number is reaching the point of diminishing returns.

Although rare, some learning experiences and opportunities to share information online can be unlimited. While these spaces can quickly become very noisy places, there are times when a fully open and unlimited exploration of a particular content area, idea, or question might be in order. These situations work most effectively when the focus is on a specific topic and the goal is to generate many ideas and perspectives. For example, a facilitator of the NEA Professional Practice Communities might want to lead an open discussion about implementing formative assessments in the classroom, keys to effective student discipline, or prevention of bullying.

It is important to offer a distinction and a caution at this point in the chapter. Members of a PLC are committed to *learning* together—to seeking out and building shared knowledge about the most promising practices and strategies. They seek information and evidence and avoid simply pooling unsubstantiated opinions. Even in the open and unlimited exploration of a topic, members must do more than solicit views; they must foster a results orientation by searching for compelling evidence of effectiveness. Figure 3.11 further describes the dimension of size.

Size: Kate's Scenario

Kate chose an unlimited structure for this collaboration. While technically she never imagined people from outside the district participating in the dialogue, she also never said they couldn't. Given the intimacy of the learning experience she was hoping for, Kate would have been better off establishing a limit to the size of this group, allowing her to communicate more directly with participants, perhaps organize some face-to-face interactions, and ensure that participants truly understood the purpose of their commitment.

10. Management: Direct, Facilitative, or Minimal

In those instances in which educators are merely attempting to solicit information and ideas rather than committing to the interdependence, common goals, and mutual accountability of a true

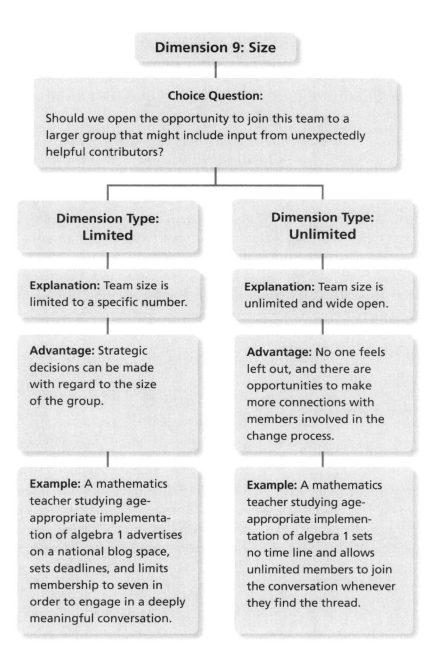

Figure 3.11: Dimension 9—size.

collaborative team, questions of leadership may not come into play. For example, if educators form a team to gather a variety of assessment tools regarding a particular content area, participants may simply post their contributions for the consideration of the team. In this case, there is little need for leadership or coordination, and it may not be necessary to designate someone as "in charge."

In other virtual learning spaces, more control is required. Teams within a face-to-face PLC meeting work most effectively when their meetings are organized, protocol driven, and facilitated by a leader or leaders. This facilitative leadership style is often collegial in nature and designed to keep participants on track, encourage broader levels of participation, guide the team away from moments of distraction, and ultimately (and skillfully) offer direction as a means for encouraging the most direct pursuit of the team's objective. Leadership competency demonstrated in face-to-face meetings in PLCs is also an effective approach for virtual teams trying to create meaningful learning opportunities. In addition, there are occasions when effective school leaders must insist that certain elements of the PLC process are honored. We explore specific strategies for team leadership in chapter 8. Figure 3.12 further describes the dimension of management.

Management: Kate's Scenario

In this case, Kate's management was quite minimal. She clearly would have benefited from a facilitative approach, in which she could provide direction without necessarily hampering the creative process. By engineering collaboration expectations at the onset, Kate could have facilitated a wonderfully dynamic discussion that allowed the process itself to generate innovations and new levels of understanding.

To review more examples of how to apply the ten dimensions for engineering a strategic e-connection, see the "Four Examples of Organizing Virtual Teams" on pages 164–171. You may also visit **go.solution-tree.com/PLCbooks** to download reproducible versions of these examples.

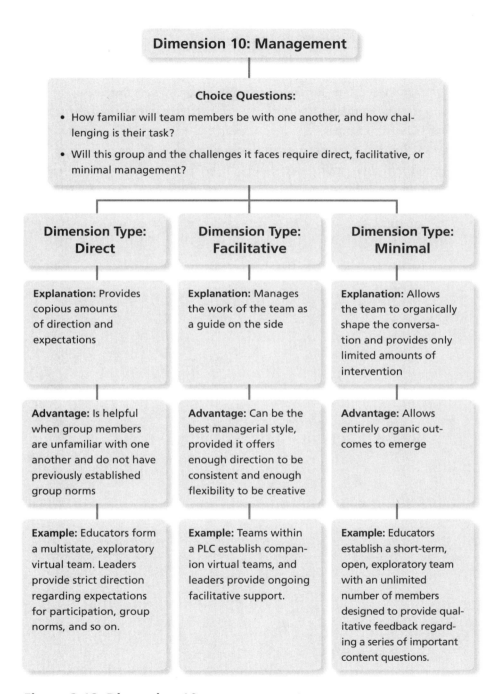

Dimension 10: Management

Choice Questions:
- How familiar will team members be with one another, and how challenging is their task?
- Will this group and the challenges it faces require direct, facilitative, or minimal management?

Dimension Type: Direct

Explanation: Provides copious amounts of direction and expectations

Advantage: Is helpful when group members are unfamiliar with one another and do not have previously established group norms

Example: Educators form a multistate, exploratory virtual team. Leaders provide strict direction regarding expectations for participation, group norms, and so on.

Dimension Type: Facilitative

Explanation: Manages the work of the team as a guide on the side

Advantage: Can be the best managerial style, provided it offers enough direction to be consistent and enough flexibility to be creative

Example: Teams within a PLC establish companion virtual teams, and leaders provide ongoing facilitative support.

Dimension Type: Minimal

Explanation: Allows the team to organically shape the conversation and provides only limited amounts of intervention

Advantage: Allows entirely organic outcomes to emerge

Example: Educators establish a short-term, open, exploratory team with an unlimited number of members designed to provide qualitative feedback regarding a series of important content questions.

Figure 3.12: Dimension 10—management.

Conclusion

Awareness of and attention to the challenges of virtual teams, and the ten dimensions for engineering and organizing those teams, are important elements in creating a supportive environment for the virtual team process. When educators make thoughtful, purposeful decisions to address those ten dimensions, they increase the likelihood that their efforts to expand collaboration to the virtual world will succeed. In the next chapter, we examine how to help virtual teams move to Level 2 of implementation by utilizing strategies for e-collaboration.

CHAPTER 4

Strategizing for e-Collaboration

Kate sat staring at her computer screen. She had called Charles, her technology coordinator, and was waiting for him to return from a boating adventure so he could log in and take down what had become a disastrous attempt at virtual collaboration in her district. While she waited for Charles, she read through some additional posts regarding ELs.

Tammy, one of Kate's favorite new teachers, had gone off on a tangent in this shared learning space about her frustrations in housebreaking her two new beagles, Lucy and Charlie Brown. She had posted pictures of the dogs and found humor in their disapproving reactions to her boyfriend. Following the thread were a number of unflattering comments that made the most of the relative juxtaposition of men and barking dogs. To make matters worse, Kate noticed that one of her staff members had taken the opportunity to post her frustration with a particularly problematic student, whom she referred to by name, as well as the girl's older brother, who had likewise been difficult to handle.

Douglas, one of the high school's social studies teachers, who came to the district just a year before Kate arrived, took advantage of this opportunity to post a long series of thoughts regarding the plight of the immigrant student and the roles of language and culture and the flattening powers of technology as variables that might shape the nation's march toward mid-21st century assimilation. He clearly expected that his missive would receive thoughtful feedback from his colleagues. When they failed to respond, he followed up twenty-four hours later with another post, which simply said, ". . . ?" Knowing Douglas, Kate could hear his wheels spinning. He was clearly frustrated that no one took the time to respond to his passionate six-page post.

In the previous chapter, we discussed the fact that one of the basic mistakes Kate made was failing to engineer a collaborative space designed to elicit productive levels of communication within the virtual team process. In addition to these Level 1 strategies, those who organize virtual teaming must also attend to Level 2 considerations, which involve strategies for e-collaboration. These strategies refer to the specific approaches, protocols, and performance expectations that must be established if collaborative learning spaces are to produce the best opportunities for teams to collaborate and learn. Even if Kate had strategically engineered the collaborative space in a more thoughtful way, the lack of adherence to these best-practice e-collaboration strategies threatened to derail meaningful progress. In this chapter, we address the strategies for e-collaboration and specifically describe how applying these strategies can help educators get the most out of their virtual teams.

The Big Picture

In order to successfully utilize virtual learning spaces to stay connected and take collaboration within a PLC to new levels, some specific strategies must be followed. Before introducing these strategies, however, there are four important big-picture issues about e-collaboration to keep in mind.

1. The PLC process is still the focus.

2. Collaboration is about people and process, not the platform.

3. Social media can affect online interaction.

4. Virtual collaborative spaces are not hack-proof.

The PLC Process Is Still the Focus

Virtual learning teams must remain faithful to the PLC process even when working online. This is true of school-based teams within a PLC utilizing virtual teaming to enhance their work. It is also true of any experimental or virtual team organized for a specific term, perhaps created in pursuit of a specific learning goal or objective. Remaining doggedly faithful to the PLC process, and the commitment to working as a team, creates greater levels of consistency and focus and better outcomes.

Every collaborative team in a PLC must constantly link its work back to the mission, vision, collective commitments, and goals that serve as the foundation of the PLC process. With virtual teams, this foundation is particularly important. Members must have processes in place to remind them of their promises to one another and the shared goals that require their collective efforts in order to be achieved. Every meeting should be purposeful in advancing the work of the team. When it comes to reminders about purpose, commitments, goals, and core elements of the PLC process, redundancy is a virtue.

Remember that the primary objective is excellent implementation of the PLC process. The use of virtual teaming and virtual collaboration is one of the tools of the trade to help make that process more powerful and effective.

Collaboration Is About People and Process, Not the Platform

The platforms that we use and the technology that enhances our collaboration continue to evolve. As soon as this book is published, there undoubtedly will be innovations taking place to change a team's capacity to connect and improve what it means to create a virtual learning space. However, no matter how many of these iterations occur in terms of virtual learning platforms, it is absolutely essential that participants remember that collaboration is about people and process, not the platform or technology used to achieve the goal.

Teams have certainly been derailed by the technological bulkiness of a particular platform or the lack of certain tools that make connection easier, and leaders of virtual teams should continue to strive for improved learning platforms. They should not, however, make platform challenges the focus of the team. Teams must use the platforms available to them today, use the PLC process to grow and evolve as teams, and strive continuously to improve their ability to operate as teams.

One of the simplest ways a team can demonstrate this commitment is to accept the bumps and flaws of any platform it is using and continue to focus on the opportunity to collaborate. Over the years, we have observed some virtual teams experience minor anomalies of a learning platform or frustrations associated with virtual engagement, wherein these issues became the focal point of complaints. Anyone reading this book has undoubtedly experienced the frustrations of imperfect technology. However, keeping the focus first and foremost on the goals of the team and the people involved in the collaboration is time better spent than on searching for the next best generation of technology.

Social Media Can Affect Online Interaction

One of the unique advantages of working online is that we can collaborate from anywhere. With virtual teams, a busy mother can connect with her iPad and participate in an asynchronous learning opportunity while waiting for her children to finish a gymnastics lesson. A busy coach can find a resource on her smartphone and link it to the group just before going to bed.

While all these opportunities to connect are signs of progress, educators also must be mindful of the unique challenges created by ever-expanding access to technology. When people are working from their cars, coffee shops, or their homes, they must fight the tendency to replace a professional learning context with a context of interaction driven by the informality or freedom of social media. Reports have surfaced about educators making ill-advised posts on Facebook or engaging in inappropriate relationships with colleagues or students as revealed in an online picture or post (Atkeson, 2014). In most cases, these interactions occurred at offline hours when the educators were in a more informal social context and, therefore, overlooked the need for professional levels of communication. Perhaps these educators would not have made those damaging Facebook comments, posts, or Instagram blasts had they been sitting in their classrooms under the auspices of the professional surroundings of their schools.

To overcome this challenge, teams must be mindful that these collaborative learning spaces are indeed meant for professional learning. Members can certainly have fun online, and we encourage them to do so. Humor and collegial interaction can create a fun context for learning. However, this expression shouldn't go too far. Erring on the side of caution, especially in a virtual learning space where misunderstandings can emerge, is a safer route to take. Had Kate implemented this strategy early, she might not have had pictures of beagles and discussions of women's ability to sort out suitable men in the learning space intended to develop strategies for serving her growing EL population. While the jokes about beagles and men may have indeed resulted in some howling laughter (please forgive us), the message demeaning men doesn't contribute to a positive learning environment and can create confusion regarding the professional context a collaborative space is designed to support.

Virtual Collaborative Spaces Are Not Hack-Proof

Educators should assume that any space in which they are working together, posting information, and reflecting could be hacked by somebody from the outside. In 2014, 5.6 percent of cyberattacks were aimed at education targets (Passeri, 2015). Students, for example, may be interested in procuring a copy of a test or seeing a sample of potential test questions on upcoming exams. Community members desirous of embarrassing the district or a particular teacher may utilize hacking skills to get into these private learning spaces and wreak havoc. The steps technology experts take to prevent hacking often lag behind systems to hack. Therefore, keep hacking in mind as you enter into team conversations, and reflect on the potential for outside eyes to view what is being said or posted.

Seven Strategies for Thoughtful Threaded Conversations

In this section, we present seven strategies that, if used consistently, help create asynchronous collaborative spaces that are full of rich, meaningful expressions, leading to new team discoveries and innovations. While these seven strategies are fairly simple to implement, they have a significant impact on the types of conversations that emerge and the level of creativity that results. These seven strategies include the following.

1. Make connections first, and then collaborate.

2. Remain private, and respect privacy.

3. Maintain appropriate commentary length.

4. Commit to active involvement, and encourage others.

5. Ask for clarification and deeper analysis.

6. Share sources and links.

7. Avoid declarations of right or wrong.

Make Connections First, and Then Collaborate

When forming a new team, people typically begin by establishing a social connection. They make eye contact and develop social ties before they focus on the work at hand. This is an instinctual reaction in which human beings engage as a mechanism for creating higher levels of interdependence (Achterman & Loertscher, 2008). When people come together, they quickly examine the safety and security of their surroundings and attempt to read their colleagues. The more accurately they are able to assess the situation, the more likely they are to identify problems ahead of time and make adjustments accordingly. This is what it means to be human, and unfortunately, this social context can prove difficult to establish online.

The need for this social interaction has led to dramatic increases in the use of services such as Skype, FaceTime, GTM, and other tools for creating more authentic human connections in which team members see each other's facial expressions rather than rely solely on voice- or text-based interactions. As a result, members of virtual teams should consider the following when attempting to make connections.

When educators walk into a face-to-face team meeting in their school, they can observe colleagues and begin to establish a sense of their levels of engagement, awareness, and comfort. For example, we tend to notice things like body language, facial expressions, and preparedness. All these subtle clues can tell us about a person's mood and give us cues as to how we should interact when we get together. Unfortunately, virtual teams don't have this advantage, and therefore, team members must make a conscious effort to establish a sense of connection and make sure that team members are aware of our moods and intentions. In fact, in most cases, it is advantageous to somewhat exaggerate your attempts to communicate this information to avoid misinterpreting mood or message. Examples of these ideas include the following.

- **Use people's names.** In both virtual and face-to-face interactions, people love to hear their names being utilized. To establish a stronger connection and create a friendly context for interaction, members of virtual teams should address one another by name.

- **Be mindful of punctuation.** Use punctuation that reflects your mood. If you are enthusiastic about something, use exclamation marks to help readers understand your message. Recently, while at a coffee shop, Casey heard two women talking about a text one of them had received from a man she obviously was hoping to get to know a little better. He had responded to one of her messages with three exclamation marks. The women were actually counting the exclamation marks because they interpreted each extra mark as an indication of his level of interest. In that virtual transaction, punctuation clearly mattered!!! It matters with virtual teams as well.

- **Say "hello," "thank you," and so on.** When connecting in a virtual learning space, it is important to once again think about how you would interact with others if you were meeting face to face. Starting off a conversation with a friendly greeting goes a long way in setting the right tone. Concluding your statement with a "thank you" or some sort of affable conclusion helps to keep the interaction upbeat and personal.

- **Check for errors.** When educators make a mistake in a virtual learning space, it hangs there for everyone to see. This can be particularly dangerous as technology attempts to correct spelling, perhaps leaving a new word that makes little sense if left uncorrected after proofreading. Educators must remember that whatever they post is literally written in their own voice. When somebody reads the post, reflection, or thread, he or she is imagining your voice behind those words. Misspelled or unintended words within the text can obscure or detract from the message, so educators should review posts carefully before submitting them to others.

- **Be careful when using icons and abbreviations.** It is important that members of a virtual team use icons effectively. Icons can convey the emotion behind a message. For example, which message would you rather receive from your virtual team leader?

  > Reminder: The report is due at 2:00pm.
  >
  > Reminder: The report is due at 2:00pm. ☺
  >
  > REMINDER: THE REPORT IS DUE AT 2:00PM!

As stated earlier, we tend to look for emotional set points in others as we try to communicate. If we don't recognize set points in written correspondence, we could assume the worst. In fact, to some people, the lack of establishing an emotional set point with words, abbreviations, or greetings might be interpreted as a cold shoulder or an exclusive focus on tasks and disinterest in personal relationships.

Educators also must be careful with abbreviations. In many cases, abbreviations may not be familiar to those who are receiving them. Several years ago, while working with a group of educators in a virtual learning space, Casey discovered that one of the learners responded to a funny comment from a colleague by writing *lmfao*. He explained to that learner, a faith-filled southern lady with great enthusiasm for students, that according to Internet slang, her abbreviation had referenced both the "F word" and her own posterior. To her embarrassment, that profanity had hung in the asynchronous space for a full day before she took it down. While there is a funny element to this story, the moral is don't rely on abbreviations, particularly when there isn't absolute clarity regarding the exact meaning.

Remain Private, and Respect Privacy

This suggestion gets at the very real habit of some people who share too much information online about themselves and the people around them. It also is important because educators must remember that these learning spaces are generally subject to Freedom of Information Act requests. Put another way, educators should not post anything in these public spaces that they wouldn't feel comfortable having a community member read aloud at a board meeting.

This particular suggestion for e-collaboration calls on educators to maintain appropriate decorum. They should not share inappropriate amounts of information about themselves or their students. In fact, they should refrain from identifying particular students by name. Addressing general trends in student behavior or academic performance at certain levels is certainly fine. Diagnosing family problems about a particular student or describing other personal issues simply shouldn't be done online.

Finally, sharing too much can have a chilling effect on the willingness of others to communicate. When people share too much, readers are often uncertain how to respond. In the worst-case scenario, people chime in with their own tales of woe, and suddenly, the learning space is transformed into an indulgent, cathartic process of oversharing. Other times, no one responds and crickets chirp, creating a socially awkward situation for all participants.

Educators must recognize that careers have been altered because people shared too much in virtual spaces. Angry, vitriolic, or insensitive postings can be destructive, and a team that is looking out for the welfare of its members might redirect its colleague to the focus and goals of its collective effort.

As is true with managing people, it is almost always inappropriate to punish people in public. For example, once while interacting in a virtual learning space, Casey noticed that a participant seemed to be increasingly agitated. Her responses to questions within the threaded dialogue were short and rather abrupt. As the days progressed, her responses began to sound irritated and angry. At one point, she explicitly questioned the professionalism of one of her colleagues. Casey recognized the need for intervention but also knew he had to counterbalance the need to intervene with the priority of making sure he did so in a way that the individual didn't lose face or feel humiliated.

In a situation like this, it is essential to reach out to make a connection, diagnose the situation, and help work through the problem to find a solution. The best course of action in this context is typically to take that conversation offline. If possible, the meeting to address the problem should be face to face. If such a meeting is not possible, consider using Skype or another tool for visual interaction.

In this example, the individual was having an extremely difficult week personally. Exhaustion and distractions led her to take out her frustrations on her teammates. By connecting with her offline and determining the issue, Casey was able to help her correct her interactions and move forward in a positive way without calling her out in front of her colleagues.

There may be times when an inappropriate post should be removed immediately rather than left hanging in virtual space. Just as a thoughtful school leadership team removes graffiti that is degrading or demeaning, negative or disempowering posts of this nature should be removed as well.

We also must remember to respect people's privacy. To that end, it is inappropriate to share the thoughts, ideas, or opinions of others without their permission. When educators share the thoughts, ideas, or opinions of others in a virtual learning space, they must ensure that their citations are accurate. Misrepresentation of authors, scholars, and research occurs far too frequently in education. For example, Marzano's (2009) research on high-yield teaching strategies was frequently used as a checklist for teacher supervision, as many readers interpreted his findings as stipulating that these were the only effective strategies or that they were universally effective. This tendency to misrepresent his conclusions led him to publish an article to set the record straight. He writes:

> The lesson to be learned is that educators must always look to whether a particular strategy is producing the desired results as opposed to simply assuming that if a strategy is being used, positive results will ensue. If a strategy doesn't appear to be working well, educators must adapt the strategy as needed or use other strategies. This is yet another reason why teachers shouldn't be required to use specific strategies. Since none are guaranteed to work, teachers must have the freedom and flexibility to adapt or try something different when student learning isn't forthcoming. (Marzano, 2009, p. 35)

Members of a PLC must be certain to avoid presenting misinformation to their colleagues. Bad information may lead to bad decisions. Educators also must avoid sharing their colleagues' thoughts and ideas without their colleagues' explicit permission. The same person who is willing to share an idea or opinion in a personal email may strongly object to that same email being posted to a collaborative learning space. The sense of trust necessary for collaboration can be badly damaged if a message intended for an audience of one is shared with an audience of many without the author's approval.

Maintain Appropriate Commentary Length

In the scenario that opened this chapter, Douglas violated the very foundation of what it means to collaborate and connect online. In a social context, Douglas had the sensibility to monitor his own airtime and avoid dominating the dialogue. Unfortunately, when it comes to virtual collaborative spaces, participants like Douglas don't always apply that filter. In Douglas's case, he thoroughly enjoys the writing process and synthesizing a multitude of ideas, responding on the thread with lengthy commentary about the plight of immigrant students. But part of good writing is keeping the audience and the purpose in mind. There is a significant difference between expressing thoughts and ideas in lengthy, scholarly, formal expository writing and the conciseness of writing to present ideas in a virtual space. While Douglas might have seen his post as an opportunity to present a mini paper, his colleagues are likely to view his verbiage as an attempt to dominate the discussion or as an opportunity to filibuster to prove his point or win an argument.

From the standpoint of social media, a blog space offers a more appropriate forum for Douglas's essay. He could then invite his team to review the blog and assess his thinking. If his goal is to create a thoughtful discussion, allowing all participants to learn something new and potentially synthesize the information, he should either create a different format to elicit reflection and conversation or synthesize his salient points to better fit with the team's learning space. Although the complexity of the topic and the interest of participants play a role in making these decisions, limiting posts to two or three paragraphs in a learning space is a good rule of thumb.

Commit to Active Involvement, and Encourage Others

Collaborating in an asynchronous learning space is not unlike going to a party—no one wants to be the first one in the room. Furthermore, if a party is quiet, it usually requires committed engagement on the part of enthusiastic partygoers to get the conversation started. To a great extent, this social dynamic is true in virtual learning spaces as well. Generally speaking, there's nothing more discouraging to a virtual learner/collaborator than to log in and see that there is very little discussion going on. The lack of activity is analogous to a party that simply hasn't started yet. Specific steps to get the party started might include the following.

- **Check in consistently.** While the PLC process calls for teams to develop their own specific norms and protocols, we highly recommend that one of those commitments include the promise to check the space within a designated timeframe. Perhaps the commitment would be to check the space at least two or three times a week and, with each visit, make some contribution. That contribution could come in the form of a response to another person's discussion or perhaps a commitment to creating an original post. Honoring this commitment has a positive effect on the team because members are much more likely to participate if they see that others are responding to what they say.

- **Elicit responses from everyone.** One of the many advantages of discussion boards for virtual teams is that they can create a sense of equity among participants. Equity is enhanced when thoughts and ideas trump longevity, gender, size, and voice. Therefore, participants should encourage everyone to make meaningful contributions. Sometimes those quiet voices on the team are more comfortable in a virtual collaborative space where they don't have to fight for airtime in a conversation. Encouraging others to actively engage and communicate their thinking is everyone's job on a team.

- **Ask everyone to commit to promoting collaboration.** While your team may assign specific responsibilities in terms of facilitation and leadership, in a truly dynamic virtual learning space, every team member is committed to creating a rich, authentic, and dynamic environment. Promoting and enforcing the rules described here should be the responsibility of every team member. Drawing out the thoughtful opinions of others, helping avoid what could be crippling mistakes, and enforcing the rules of etiquette are everyone's responsibilities. The quality of this learning space is determined by the commitment of each member to making the space a positive learning environment for all.

- **Make sure every post elicits at least one or more responses.** Virtual learning spaces have a way of sorting out good ideas from those that are less promising. Teams should agree, however, that any idea submitted warrants at least some response. Every member of the virtual team should commit to ensuring that no original post in a discussion space is allowed to hang without some level of feedback or at least acknowledgment of the issue. This creates the expectation that ideas are honored and all thoughts are considered. Failure to make this commitment can give the impression that less-worthy ideas are punished by being ignored.

Ask for Clarification and Deeper Analysis

As mentioned before, it is extraordinarily helpful to provide at least some feedback to every initial thread posted. This motivates members to engage fully, knowing that their words are read. One of the most powerful steps participants can take to ensure active engagement in this process is to ask for clarification or to present probing questions when an important point is presented. If, for example, a member of a team posts an interesting strategy for engaging students early in a lesson, asking for clarification or further illustrations can strengthen the dialogue. The inquiry could generate curiosity in other members who may have only glanced at the thread. It could inspire the person who initiated the post to be more thoughtful regarding his or her own instructional practice and the evidence of learning supporting that practice. It could lead to the entire team launching an action research project to test its colleague's hypothesis.

A word of warning, however: team members should not seek clarification or ask for a deeper analysis if they really don't want it. If an idea posted doesn't stimulate curiosity, participants shouldn't ask for clarification just to be nice. Ideas that aren't particularly strong or moving shouldn't be patronized by insincere requests for clarification. As stated previously, team members should honor the work of others and acknowledge everyone's contributions. Not every idea, however, is worthy of exploration and deep analysis. That is the reality of adult learners working in a collaborative space. But when ideas generate genuine interest, seeking clarification and presenting probing questions only improve the quality of teamwork.

Share Sources and Links

Sharing sources, links, or other resources also is a very powerful way to create a more dynamic learning environment. If participants recognize that one of the important steps in building shared knowledge is to bring sources to the learning space, members begin to see these spaces as more beneficial and meaningful. If, for example, a team of teachers tries to discover an effective approach to teaching a particularly difficult concept, members could post a series of links, video demonstrations, and other tools for the group to consider. Through discussion threads, reflection, and ultimately some experimentation, teams could begin to use these sources and reflect on their impact on students. The other advantage of utilizing virtual learning spaces for this type of work is that it is much easier to catalog resources, keep them organized, and continue to apply them in a thoughtful and focused way.

Avoid Declarations of Right or Wrong

In order for quality online learning experiences to emerge, participants must feel safe enough to take risks, experiment, and openly inquire about ideas they aren't familiar with. The presence of toxic interactions, negativity, or the compulsion to prove oneself right and others wrong significantly diminishes the quality of team interactions, particularly in a virtual team. A snarky or sarcastic comment in a meeting can create an awkward moment, but that same comment in a virtual space can hang around forever and be repeated numerous times in threaded conversation. In this situation, the wound is difficult to heal.

Effective teams avoid declaring winners or losers or focusing on proving a colleague to be "dead wrong" about an idea he or she shares. They recognize that engaging in collective inquiry is vital to the PLC process, and intellectual curiosity and openness to others' ideas are essential elements of collective inquiry.

It is equally true, however, that the PLC process is intended to build shared knowledge rather than merely pool opinions. Not every idea is a good idea, and assertions shared without evidence should be addressed. We recognize that we are calling for a delicate balance here. On the one hand, team members should be open to the ideas of others; but on the other hand, the team is seeking to identify promising practices that are grounded in evidence.

Peter Senge and colleagues (1994) offer a useful protocol for addressing this dilemma. Rather than simply dismissing a colleague's assertion as wrong, consider the following.

- Ask your colleague to present the evidence and examples that support the assertion.

- Use unaggressive language such as "Help me understand" rather than "What do you mean?"

- Draw out your colleague's reasoning to understand why he or she is making the assertion.

- Explain your reasoning for presenting questions.

- Compare your assumptions and evidence to your colleague's. Where do you have common ground, and where do you differ?

- Ask for broader contexts or examples of his or her assumptions at work.

- Check your understanding of what your colleague said.

Once team members become accustomed to the fact that they will be asked to present evidence to support their proposals as a routine part of the team process, the team is far more likely to focus on building shared knowledge rather than pooling opinions.

For example, several years ago, Casey was working in a virtual learning space where participants were discussing the psychological safety of today's schools. Several participants contributed to a thread that reinforced their perception that schools were more dangerous than ever. Perpetual 24/7 news alerts notwithstanding, the hype around school violence is different from the reality. The statistics are clear that over the past generation, schools have gotten increasingly safer (Robers, Kemp, Rathbun, Morgan, & Snyder, 2014). The number of violent acts in all areas has decreased.

Casey responded by honoring the interest of participants in keeping schools safe and then presented the relevant statistics. Instead of using the data to declare them wrong, he stated the facts, cited the source, and then presented a series of questions, such as, How do you interpret the data? What are the implications? Is there good news when it comes to school safety? The focus was on building shared knowledge rather than on declaring that others were wrong.

Conclusion

No team should be expected to master all these strategies at once. Becoming skillful in applying them is a work in progress. However, consistent application significantly enhances the climate and culture of all the interactions that happen both in virtual space and face to face.

After carefully engineering the e-connection (Level 1) and then thoughtfully embracing and applying the strategies of e-collaboration (Level 2), new opportunities for adult learning should emerge. In the best-case scenario, with practice, these process points ultimately lead to the development of new individual and team capacities, as well as a significantly improved capacity to establish, maintain, and apply heightened levels of shared knowledge. In the next chapter, we address additional steps teams can take to further enhance team learning through strategies of e-acceleration (Level 3).

CHAPTER 5

Enhancing Learning With e-Acceleration

When Rick took a typing class in high school, the class utilized the most advanced technology available at the time—manual typewriters. Years later, when he wrote his dissertation—an historical study of female students from Boston public schools—the typist he hired had the advantage of an electronic typewriter. To do the necessary research for his study, Rick spent weeks in the Boston Public Library combing through documents, records, and books. As he submitted chapters to his dissertation committee for review, the committee frequently felt compelled to seek more information or suggest the incorporation of additional resources. Several of their recommendations required him to make more trips from Chicago to Boston in search of a resource. Each revision or addition to a chapter meant the entire chapter had to be retyped from that point. The approved dissertation was more than 400 pages, but the typist had completed almost 1,200 pages in order to provide the finished product.

With the advent of word processing, the archaic, time-consuming, repetitive process of retyping was replaced with the convenience of cutting and pasting into a single text. Even more important, however, was the fact that the information needed to complete such a study no longer required trips to the library and combing through the stacks. The Internet puts information on virtually any subject at the researcher's fingertips. These new tools, and the advantages they offer, have transformed both the writing and research processes.

Not unlike the transformation from typewriters to personal computers (PCs), and access to all that is available on the Internet, today's collaborative teams are utilizing the power and potential of technology to improve the PLC process, reaching far beyond school walls to connect with outside sources. This era of openness and access to external information and support from outside the school is changing how collaborative teams go about their work.

This chapter presents the Level 3 strategies for enhancing learning with e-acceleration. We were quite purposeful in choosing *acceleration* to describe this level of virtual collaboration. The goal always revolves around the pursuit of new innovations, improved team capacities, and the outcomes they produce. Today, we have the power to accelerate the innovation capacities of PLC teams by more thoughtfully using outside innovative sources and the potential wisdom of the virtual crowd to inspire the collective imaginations and contributions of teams within a PLC. Currently, many schools simply don't reach out to available voices in virtual spaces. And if they do, those attempts are disjointed at best. In this chapter, we explore a more disciplined approach for accelerating the learning and innovative influence of PLC teams by demonstrating how to utilize the power that's available in virtual open spaces.

Openness: A Philosophical Transformation

In the early days of the Internet, the term *openness* described the ability of one mainframe computer to talk to another and transpose information. This leap forward in technology introduced the madness and majesty of sharing at the speed of light (Bonk, 2009).

Today, users not only are open to other users but also web resources, software downloads to enhance their work, and any number of other outside resources that would be unavailable without the technology and philosophy of openness that drive users out into the open.

While much is made in the media about the emerging tools that make openness possible, the most powerful transformation of openness occurs around the philosophical shift that it brings to users. Therefore, for the purpose of enhancing virtual teaming in a PLC, we use *openness* to refer to the philosophy of enhancing individual and team learning by utilizing technology to challenge old paradigms; reach out beyond local boundaries; and transform how teams think, learn, and innovate.

Getting Open: A Scenario

Joyce had been teaching middle school science for twenty-five years. Her school embraced the PLC concept, and her team was interested in trying to identify some schoolwide STEM (science, technology, engineering, and mathematics) projects to help integrate the subjects in an authentic way. She and her team also wanted to engage the support of tech-related business and industry, but they were not sure how to get started. Tim, a colleague who had been teaching for five years, agreed to help her with her search and keep their team informed of their progress.

Tim got started on Facebook, where he found several very active STEM pages and joined them. One of the pages had a pop-up reminder that he had five other Facebook friends in this group. He reached out to them through Facebook to seek help with the work of his team, but none of them was able to offer information on an effective schoolwide STEM project that included local businesses.

Tim then returned to the STEM Facebook pages and noticed that there were almost four hundred teachers actively participating in these spaces. From reading some of their posts, he was able to identify several teachers who appeared to engage local business and industry in their work. One teacher from Pennsylvania had written a blog on the topic that referenced a Thomas Friedman editorial. Tim decided to participate on the blog and asked several questions related to STEM project integration. Within twenty-four hours, a teacher from California provided him with some very informative feedback and links to several West Coast websites. He also was lucky enough to find some interesting resources, including sample lesson plans and guidelines to communicating with parents about STEM. One of those resources pointed Tim toward a STEM page on Pinterest that offered a number of interesting STEM education policy documents and some leads on STEM grant funding.

Joyce took a slightly different approach. She searched YouTube for related content and found a fascinating mini lecture from a teacher in Florida named Myron. His YouTube channel was filled with wonderfully helpful lesson-plan ideas and even some samples of lesson execution. Myron referenced another Florida educator named Stefan, who didn't have his own YouTube channel, but he posted a number of times on Myron's channel. In addition to featuring some interesting video content, Stefan made a number of thoughtful observations in reaction to Myron's videos. With some additional digging, Joyce found that Stefan blogged extensively on the topic and posted a number of references and resources she found relevant to their work.

Joyce decided to reach out to Stefan on LinkedIn. They were soon connected and began to exchange messages through the LinkedIn portal. Stefan also connected Joyce to one of his many Twitter feeds. He had created a Twitter group specifically related to STEM-integrated projects. By following this group, Joyce was able to access a thread of previous posts, evaluate dozens of additional links, meet scores of educators (several of whom were from outside the United States), and ask direct questions of a group of educators that was in a great position to provide her with feedback.

Getting Open: The Results

When Joyce and Tim rejoined their synchronous, face-to-face team in their school, they had a lot to share. In a short period of time, they had made authentic, highly interactive connections with a number of professionals who provided helpful input; gathered sources; observed teachers doing the work of a schoolwide STEM project; and examined threaded discussions that helped them glean some of the arguments, challenges, and solutions other educators discovered when engaged in this work. This infusion of learning gave Joyce and Tim a tremendous amount of enthusiasm for what they were studying and clarity about what it would take to make progress. Their school-based teammates were grateful for their work and were eager to integrate it into their program. The team discovered the benefits of being open to ideas and information beyond its school, and members began contributing to the groups that were so helpful to them. From that point forward, the work of the team shifted from a focus on engaging solely with one another to a focus on accessing the expertise of others beyond the walls of the school.

From Convenience to Creativity

Openness does more than enhance the convenience of virtual teaming. It encourages a shift from viewing the Internet as electronic Yellow Pages to seeing it instead as an interactive learning space where thoughts can be presented, sensibilities challenged, information gathered, and revolutions ignited. The hallmark of openness in schools is the recognition that the answers to the most difficult questions regarding school improvement come both from the work of collaborative teams within a PLC (the inside) and the innovative forces and creative energies available in a truly open environment (the outside).

Wisdom From the Field

The era of openness on the web has created an opportunity for sharing new levels of wisdom and expertise from the field. In the previous example, Joyce and Tim made choices based on the merits and wisdom of the people or groups they found. The teachers they interacted with were not formal researchers. None of them had ever written a book. Some were prolific bloggers, and several appeared at a few state and regional conferences. What they offered, however, was the ability to contribute to the conversation based on their first-hand experience and deeper learning that only can occur by engaging directly in the work. This wisdom from the field in these open spaces allows participants to gather new insights and perspectives in developing shared knowledge within the teams and their PLCs.

From Watching and Reading to Writing and Interacting

One of the essential elements of the PLC process is the importance of maintaining an action orientation. Adults learn by doing, and taking action gives them an opportunity to apply what they learn. The technology evolution and a work environment driven by openness shift the nature of work from watching and reading to much more significant levels of action and interaction. For example, rather than just watching a video or reading a book, the open culture encourages educators to rate the content, write a review, become a follower on Twitter, "like" the post or resource on Facebook, offer a different perspective, or contact the author to clarify questions. Joyce, the twenty-five-year veteran, began her career with well-intended department chairs handing out photocopies of articles and highlighting the important points. Rarely, however, did she discuss the content with her colleagues. Today, Joyce is able to "friend" the authors of those articles and interact with fellow readers from virtually anywhere. In both instances, Joyce read articles, but the culture of openness encourages a much more engaged level of interaction.

Personal Learning Networks

Personal learning networks (PLNs) are informal networks of people who interact for an indeterminate amount of time regarding a specific topic of interest (Bonk, 2010; Digenti, 1999). Both Joyce and Tim became part of a PLN as they used tools, such as Facebook, Pinterest, YouTube, and LinkedIn, to research topics of interest, find other interested parties, and interact with the purpose of increasing their shared knowledge.

The advantages of PLNs are that they can be accessed quickly, and they do not require a long-term commitment either to the group or to the pursuit at hand. If Joyce was able to gather useful ideas for creating STEM business partnerships, she could choose to either continue to participate in helpful external groups or disengage from them. If she was unable to get the specific information she wanted, she could start a Facebook page devoted specifically to this topic. She could leave it open so others could find it and request to join. Once her questions had been answered, she could opt out of the exchange.

Similarities and Differences

Diversity can be a catalyst for innovation and breakthroughs. Joyce and Tim were able to bring perspectives to their team from educators working in very different types of schools. There also are advantages, however, to creating partnerships with similar schools. When Casey was a principal, his high school had twice as many students as any other school within one hundred miles. As a result, when he faced the challenge of solving problems unique to larger schools, he typically relied on a network of large high schools that included those many miles from his own. When a PLN is created and open-source efforts are extended, educators can find and learn from other educators working in similar environments.

Openness to Experts

Openness also creates opportunities for the speedy recovery of answers and access to information that can enhance the work of a team. Today, collaborative team meetings can be enhanced by ready access to information from a laptop or tablet. Openness also provides instantaneous access to networks of educators who respond quickly to questions, especially for members of their own PLNs whom they recognize and are dedicated to helping.

Furthermore, technology innovations make it easier to access and seek help from recognized experts in the field. Many experts who tweet respond to direct messages in their Twitter accounts from the field. They may even create a dialogue that would have been difficult to initiate or sustain without the advent of today's technology.

Leadership in the Era of Openness

In the traditional hierarchical model of schooling, those at the top of the organization served as the gatekeepers of information. The central office or, in some cases, the principal decided what information to share with teachers and what information to withhold. With the access to information and expertise that technology and open sourcing provide, this approach to management has become obsolete. Every educator can now gather information on curriculum, instruction, assessment, classroom management, and all the other factors that contribute to effective teaching. Leading in this environment demands creating structures for shared leadership and empowered teachers. We address leadership more fully in chapter 8.

Playing at a Higher Level

One of the greatest advantages of the era of openness in today's schools is direct access to high-performing teams and schools. While previous generations might have heard about these high performers by reading an article, today's educators have direct access to these outliers and are able to make critical observations of their performance. Earlier in this book, we used the example of Roger Bannister breaking a four-minute mile and its impact on raising the bar in terms of expectations. Openness and tools, such as Twitter, Facebook, and so on, would allow a modern-day Bannister to share, in a direct and personal way, his paradigm-breaking achievement and the steps he took on a daily basis to make that achievement possible. Modern, open-source tools can offer both the granular clarity that supports effective implementation of meaningful school improvement and the motivation to replicate excellence.

Is Openness Enough?

Just as gathering a group of teachers in a room does not create a PLC, starting a Twitter account and beginning to look around the web don't make a school truly open. Openness must be initiated with consistency and discipline. Choices must be made, and thoughtful steps must be taken. To reach Level 3 implementation of virtual teaming in a PLC, it is important to incorporate strategies established in Levels 1 and 2. Therefore, in the following section, we revisit the ten dimensions for engineering a strategic e-connection and apply them to the challenge of integrating openness into the team process.

1. Membership: Open or Closed

In this context, a team within a PLC has to decide whether the pursuit of outside voices would be more efficient if interested participants were "open" to join the conversation extemporaneously or the formation of a more formalized, invited outside group would be more effective. For example, Joyce and Tim's team could post its questions in a blog space, such as www.allthingsplc.info, or within the NEA Professional Practice Communities. These are both examples of open venues that allow participants from virtually all over the world to offer their professional expertise. The advantage, once again, is the opportunity to gain free-flowing information from practitioners who are familiar with the issue the sourcing school is presenting. If the topic is particularly volatile, a closed structure might be a better choice.

2. Connection: Virtual, Face to Face, or Hybrid

Because open-source strategies tend to involve voices from far beyond the local boundaries of the district, most connections are obviously virtual ones. However, a team could come together in cyberspace and stay connected using virtual platforms for a prescribed period of time. Members could then choose to enhance that connection by meeting face to face at some point, such as during the summer at a conference. Online dating is an example of this type of connection. Suitors must establish a degree of openness as it relates to procuring a date. They make a virtual connection, and the merits of that connection determine whether a face-to-face meeting is mutually agreeable.

3. Scope: Team, School, Local District, Regional/State, or National/International

Open-source strategies are, by definition, those that reach beyond the team or school level. In larger districts, a team may elect to apply open-source approaches to other schools in its district. More commonly, however, the scope of open-source strategies would be either regional/state or national/international.

While the inclusion of international voices might seem like a rather exotic step, there are some advantages to making these connections. Several years ago, Casey was able to help connect a group of high-performing early childhood educators from New Zealand with a team from the Detroit area. While the accents were different (occasional Skype calls were utilized), the delights and dilemmas were remarkably the same. Furthermore, these teachers discovered that both groups were in some ways inhibited by habits and perspectives that might never have been challenged or addressed had they not come together.

4. Format: Asynchronous, Synchronous, or Hybrid

Because open sourcing can sometimes involve making connections with individuals or groups outside of normal working hours or from varying time zones, asynchronous formats (such as Facebook and VoiceThread) are the most common choices. Synchronous virtual connections enhanced by tools, such as Skype, can be particularly impactful when establishing the initial connection. Despite the digital evolution, there never will be a substitute for putting a face with a name as collaboration begins.

5. Orientation: Grade Level / Content Area or Function

Most centralized, open-source collaborations are grade-level or content-area specific. However, school improvement teams certainly could employ these same open-source approaches and create meaningful dialogue and sharing opportunities with other schools. Virtual vertical teaming is another viable option. One of the most active and innovative groups in the NEA Professional Practice Communities is an open, K–12, vertical mathematics team that has developed and shared a variety of sources and tools for mathematics teachers at all grade levels.

6. Duration: Ongoing or Term

The work of teams within a PLC is continuous. In relation to open-source efforts, however, there may be some distinct advantages to establishing a specific and limited term. If a specific timeframe is established, outside participants recognize their commitment is for a limited duration. Having a specific deadline or term can also create a greater sense of urgency to gather and synthesize information and input and act on the results. If Tim and his team knew that a decision was imminent regarding a specific aspect of their STEM topic, they would be more inclined to set a deadline and gather the necessary information in a timely manner.

7. Origin: Planned or Unplanned

The origin of open-source connections is typically planned pursuant to the protocols previously described; however, the opportunity to engage in a thoughtful outside source could happen almost anytime. A member of a team may stumble upon an informative series of posts or tweets authored by an educator outside the team. This thoughtful, external voice could influence a team member who, in turn, could impact the entire team. Furthermore, the team might engage that educator'in an ongoing conversation to further explore his or her ideas.

8. Purpose: Ignite/Inform, Learn and Transform, or Give Voice / Send a Message

In most cases, the purpose of open sourcing is to learn something new from the outside in hopes of improving the work of the team on the inside. Pursuing open-source approaches with the purpose of igniting/informing occurs when a team is exploring a particular idea or innovation. For example, if a school is implementing the flipped classroom approach, faculty members might utilize open sourcing as a way to ignite interest in the topic or explore keys to implementation. Open sourcing that intends to give voice or send a message could evolve from serving a particular student group, such as autistic students, in which both advocacy and understanding are necessary to meet student needs.

9. Size: Limited or Unlimited

While there is conflicting research regarding appropriate numbers of participants for effective virtual team learning opportunities, the topic at hand should influence decisions about the size of a team. If the topic requires considerable professional expertise and there is an expectation that all members engage fully in its consideration, the size of the team should be smaller. If the goal is to gather as much information as possible on a more general topic, the team should cast a wider net.

Participants typically are more likely to respond positively to a focused conversation, particularly when the invitation is an acknowledgment of their expertise. If, for example, Tim and Joyce wanted intensive input on integrated lesson-plan development and identified a handful of experts from various sources, an invitation to participate in their team could be viewed as a badge of honor. Finally, it is much easier to create a greater sense of purpose, direction, and cooperation with a smaller, more intimate team than a larger one.

10. Management: Direct, Facilitative, or Minimal

Getting the most out of open-source efforts requires structure, organization, shared expectations, and carefully prescribed goals for participants. A centralized or facilitative management style may be beneficial when first establishing the open-source connection; however, the best teams soon become self-directed once initial implementation is completed.

Conclusion

When it comes to utilizing strategies in open sourcing, there is still much left to discover. One of the strongest arguments for PLC implementation is that differences in student achievement from teacher to teacher within the same school are consistently greater than the cumulative differences in student performance from one school to the next (Hattie, 2012). Critics of K–12 education might observe these findings and argue that more teacher supervision is needed so that school administrators can fire low performers more frequently. There is no empirical evidence, however, that firing teachers leads to improved levels of performance (Baker, et al., 2010). Furthermore, firing the worst teachers does nothing to improve the effectiveness of those who remain.

Yet the research suggests that within most schools, there are pockets of excellence. As we stated at the outset, the way to improve schools is to ensure more effective teaching in more classrooms more of the time. There is no shortcut. By implementing the PLC process and enlisting the collective learning power of high-performing teams, the most effective educators are able to share their expertise and help others grow from the experience. Open-source strategies as part of virtual teaming provide educators within a PLC with access to unprecedented levels of talent, ideas, resources, and professional development opportunities. When our profession fully embraces the philosophy and practices of openness, the potential for building the individual and collective capacity of its members can increase exponentially.

As John F. Kennedy once observed, "A rising tide lifts all boats." Accelerating the power of virtual teaming with open-source strategies gives educators an opportunity to lift the entire profession by tapping into their collective expertise.

CHAPTER 6

Improving School-Based Teams With Virtual Teams

There is no question that technology has played a major role in facilitating the PLC process. Shared sites have allowed teachers to discuss their conclusions about essential standards, common assessments, lesson plans, and supplementary materials. Software programs have presented teachers with user-friendly analyses of assessment results by the student and by the standard. Websites have offered assistance in reviewing standards and creating valid assessments.

One of the most exciting technology tools to support the PLC process is Global PD by Solution Tree. The program was specifically created to assist educators in exploring the critical questions of the PLC process. It offers online collaboration tools that help teams identify essential standards and translate them into student-friendly learning targets, build and score common assessments, generate charts and graphs to reveal the proficiency and needs of individual students, and monitor the effects of intervention and enrichment for students. Global PD also offers an extensive video library on every aspect of the PLC process presented by experts as a powerful online learning tool. For example, a team preparing to write its first common assessment has access to scores of brief videos from assessment experts offering keys to creating valid assessments. Finally, the program offers an ongoing, on-demand, virtual coaching program to support teams and administrators as they encounter issues or generate questions.

Despite these advances, the PLC process encounters inherent obstacles. PLCs operate from the premise that educators are more effective when they work collaboratively with others. But many teachers are singletons—the only person in his or her school assigned to teach in a particular area (such as a librarian or a reading specialist) or course. How are singletons to engage in meaningful dialogue with others regarding their curriculum, instruction, and assessments if no one shares their assignments?

Another premise of PLCs is that educators can lift students to higher levels of learning if they use common assessment results to help one another improve their instructional practice. However, what if the assessments reveal that no one on the team is successful at teaching a particular skill or concept to students?

Finally, the PLC process breaks down the walls of isolation to provide educators with access to their colleagues' expertise. But if schools replace isolated teachers with isolated teams, the potential of the PLC process will not be realized.

Virtual teams can help address these challenges. Singleton teachers can join colleagues in their district, state, or nation with the same teaching assignment and collaborate to focus on the right work, as addressed in chapter 2. Proximity does not guarantee people work collaboratively, and distance does not negate the possibility of creating a powerful collaborative team. Given the ubiquity of contemporary technology, it is disingenuous for any educator to say, "But I have no one to collaborate with." Virtual teams can solve the singleton problem.

Virtual collaboration can also expand any team's access to expertise when the team discovers all its members are experiencing difficulty in teaching a skill or concept. Members of a team in one school can link with a team in a sister school. Teams can post a question or problem to an open source and ask for input from other educators. They can access websites to explore how other educators are teaching a skill or concept. The reproducible on page 172 lists several websites that are just a few examples of the growing number of venues to which educators can turn for help. You may also visit **go.solution-tree .com/PLCbooks** to download a reproducible list of these websites.

There is no question that virtual collaboration can help address some of the challenges of the PLC process. Now, let's consider how elements of the PLC process can facilitate the creation of powerful virtual collaboration.

Powerful Team Structure

There are certainly a variety of ways to structure a virtual collaborative team. Teachers with a particular interest may elect to seek out other like-minded educators who share that interest. The unifying theme could be a passion for a topic (the Civil War), a subject area (chemistry), an approach to presenting curriculum (interdisciplinary study), the uniqueness of a situation (teaching in a small school), or an instructional strategy (cooperative learning).

The team structures that have been most effective in leading to improvement in student learning, however, are grade-level teams in elementary schools and course-specific teams in middle and high schools (Fulton & Britton, 2011; Gallimore, Ermeling, Saunders, & Goldenberg, 2009; Little & Bartlett, 2010; Saphier, King, & D'Auria, 2006). Gallimore and colleagues (2009) conclude that job-alike teams are "critical to teachers sustaining and benefitting from instructional inquiry" (p. 548). They caution that without shared goals immediately applicable to their classrooms, teams drift toward superficial discussions. In their review of the research, Judith Warren Little and Lora Bartlett (2006) agree that the adult learning with the greatest impact on teacher practice and student learning is subject-specific teaching, which is "strongly tied to the curriculum, instruction, and assessment that students would encounter" (p. 7).

We strongly recommend, therefore, that when teachers explore creating a virtual team, their first consideration should be to establish subject-area teams, such as teachers who teach third-grade language arts, algebra, eighth-grade science, and so on. It is easiest to apply the PLC process to subject-area teams. Furthermore, subject-area teams are not precluded from examining specific curricular or instructional issues for their team. A fourth-grade language arts team can explore better ways to engage students in a lesson. A U.S. history team can consider how to integrate technology into its curriculum. So our first bit of advice to those considering a virtual team structure is to establish your team based on a common grade-level curriculum.

Teams, Not Groups

Another critical early step in establishing a collaborative team is to ensure members function as a true team and not merely as a group. A group may include people with common interests or who face similar challenges. People who run in marathons are a group. They are engaged in a common challenging task as they pursue their individual goals of completing the marathon. They are not, however, a team. People who join a book club may share a common interest in reading, but they, too, are not a team. In order to meet the standard of a team, *members must work interdependently to achieve shared goals for which members are mutually accountable* (DuFour et al., 2010).

Therefore, one of the first tasks members of virtual collaborative teams must achieve is to establish one or more SMART goals based on evidence of improved student learning. Effective teams are always characterized by a common purpose and specific performance goals for which members hold themselves mutually accountable. As a comprehensive study of high-performing teams concludes:

> Those who describe teams as vehicles primarily to make people feel good or get along better not only

confuse teamwork with teams, but also miss the most
fundamental characteristic that distinguishes real teams
from nonteams—a relentless focus on performance . . .
teams and performance are inextricably connected.
(Katzenbach & Smith, 1993, pp. 21–22, 44)

As mentioned in chapter 2, it is imperative that members of a collaborative team establish a SMART goal that the team agrees to support to improve student achievement. Because members of virtual teams may be in different districts or states, each member may need to establish an individual SMART goal most relevant to his or her situation. Once again, the goal should be strategic (aligned with the school's goals), measurable, attainable, results oriented, and time bound. Goals may focus on student achievement on state or district benchmark assessments, local grade distributions, the number of students opting to pursue and succeed in the most rigorous curriculum, the percentage of students meeting proficiency standards on the Common Core assessments from the Smarter Balanced Assessment Consortium and the Partnership for Assessment of Readiness for College and Careers (PARCC), the percentage of students earning honor grades on AP exams, and so on.

Team members should observe the following guidelines.

- They must establish a goal to improve student achievement.

- They must establish one or more indicators of improvement to track for their respective students.

- They must commit to helping each member achieve his or her goal.

- They must remember that one of the greatest challenges to team success is inattention to results. The true measure of a team's success is whether it accomplishes what it set out to accomplish.

The Right Work in Virtual Teams

Once again, if a team agrees that its purpose is to promote higher levels of learning, both for team members and the students they serve, the primary focus should be directly related to student learning. Consider the following example of a process specifically designed to improve learning.

Seven teachers utilized the NEA Professional Practice Communities to establish a collaborative team. The team focus was on helping its eighth-grade students become proficient nonfiction writers. Two of the teachers were from Michigan, three were from Wisconsin, and two were from Iowa. At the beginning, members shared their reasons for joining a virtual team and established a common purpose. They also expressed their ideas about how an ideal virtual team should operate. Once this clarity regarding the purpose of the team and the ideal team they hoped to create was established, members began engaging in the following structured team-learning process.

- Members clarified their expectations of how to work together by establishing a written list of commitments to their teammates.

- They established a shared site for posting documents and comments, as well as a VoiceThread for posing questions and offering ideas on their work. Members also agreed to meet via Skype at 8:00 a.m. every Monday to engage in their work.

- The team established a SMART goal of increasing the percentage of each teacher's students who demonstrated proficiency on the Smarter Balanced writing assessment, which was to be administered toward the end of the school year.

- Each member studied the Common Core curriculum in language arts for eighth graders and asked ninth-grade teachers to identify the most important nonfiction writing skills students should master before they enter ninth grade. Members posted their findings on the team's shared site and commented on teammates' findings. They agreed that one of the first essential skills they wanted their students to demonstrate was writing a clear, coherent central claim.

- Members shared their thoughts on prerequisite skills that students must have in order to write to a central claim. They decided that the ability to identify a central claim in a writing passage was a skill that increased the likelihood of students demonstrating proficiency in writing their own central claims.

- Members gathered reading passages appropriate to the grade level and jointly developed a common preassessment to gather evidence of their students' ability to recognize the central claim in those passages.

- Each member administered the preassessment to his or her students and shared the results with teammates. Based on their joint analysis of the results, the team members concluded that some students in all schools have difficulty identifying central claims. They decided to spend a few days reviewing that skill before beginning instruction on how to write a central claim. Members shared ideas regarding the review strategies they would use.

- Prior to beginning the unit, the team studied the Smarter Balanced rubric for assessing the quality of student writing. Members made minor modifications to establish their own rubric. They agreed on the criteria to use to assess student writing for each level on their four-point rubric. They agreed that students must score at least three to be considered proficient.

- Once the team agreed on the rubric, the team facilitator provided each member with an example of a student's attempt to write a central claim. Each member was asked to apply the team's rubric to that student's writing. Members shared their scores, only to find significant differences in the ways they assessed student writing. They discussed the disparity, attempted to reestablish common ground on how to apply the rubric to student writing, and agreed to practice applying the rubric to another student's work in order to establish greater inter-rater reliability in assessing student writing.

- The team's facilitator asked different team members to develop anchor papers to represent the different scores for their rubric. Some members submitted papers that they felt warranted a score of one, others a score of two, and so on. Every member read each paper and assigned a score. They discussed differences until the team reached consensus on representative anchor papers for each score. Members were encouraged to share these anchor papers with students and point out the items that led to different scores.

- The team agreed that it would devote three weeks to teaching this unit.

- Team members considered a variety of instructional strategies they might use in their classrooms and agreed that each teacher should determine which strategies worked best for his or her students.

- The team studied writing prompts from Smarter Balanced; PARCC; the National Assessment of Educational Progress; the Programme for International Student Assessment (PISA); International Baccalaureate; Advanced Placement; Cambridge International Examinations; and other state, provincial, and international assessments. They selected a prompt from Smarter Balanced to gather evidence of student learning.

- All team members administered the writing assessment to their students on the agreed-on day.

- Each team member scored his or her student drafts according to the team rubric and shared all scores with teammates. The team facilitator also assigned each teacher to present one student's paper. Two team members each submitted a student paper that scored a one, two others submitted papers that scored twos, two others submitted papers that scored threes, and one member submitted a paper that scored a four. Each member reviewed and scored each of the seven papers, not knowing how his or her colleague originally scored it. The team members discovered that they had not yet established consistent inter-rater reliability, but they were encouraged by the fact that they were getting much closer.

- Members analyzed the collective results from the writing assignment using the data analysis protocol shown in figure 6.1 (page 122). Visit **go.solution-tree .com/PLCbooks** to download a reproducible version of this figure. You may also find the data analysis protocol at allthingsplc.info (www.allthingsplc.info /files/uploads/data_analysis_protocol.pdf).

- Members agreed that they would reinforce skills for writing a central claim in the next unit, which was designed to help students learn how to use supporting arguments for their central claims. They created an assessment for that skill and agreed to devote three weeks of instruction to the unit.

Team: _____

Teacher: _____ Date: _____

This analysis is based on our team's common assessment of the following essential learnings.

_____

_____

1. Which of our students need additional time and support to achieve at or above proficiency on an essential learning? How will we provide that time and support?

_____

_____

2. What is our plan to enrich and extend the learning for students who are highly proficient?

_____

_____

3. What is an area in which my students struggled?

_____

_____

4. What strategies were used by teammates whose students performed well?

_____

_____

5. What is an area in which the team's students struggled? What do we believe is the cause? What is our plan for improving the results?

_____

_____

Source: www.allthingsplc.info/files/uploads/data_analysis_protocol.pdf.

Figure 6.1: Data analysis protocol.

Visit **go.solution-tree.com/PLCbooks** to download a reproducible version of this figure.

This team learning process represents the essential, recursive work of collaborative teams, whether they are in brick-and-mortar or virtual settings. It is designed to create a shared understanding of what students must know and be able to do, an agreed-on process for gathering evidence of student learning, a protocol for using that evidence to inform and improve the professional practice of the team and each of its members, and the timely information necessary to respond to individual student needs.

Notice that the process empowers teachers to make key decisions. Teachers work collaboratively to answer the questions of what to teach, how to teach, how to pace the content, how to assess student learning, what criteria to use in judging the quality of student work, the standard students must meet in order to be considered proficient, and what the evidence of student learning reveals about effective instructional practice.

Teams certainly benefit from other discussions as well. Members may seek the advice of their peers on such topics as getting students to complete homework, evaluating individual students when working in cooperative groups, addressing off-task behavior, finding well-designed supplementary materials, or meeting the needs of a student who struggles with dyslexia. There is no question that these conversations can prove to be invaluable. However, if the team never moves beyond sharing classroom management tips, helpful materials, and instructional strategies; or if the team doesn't use the collective analysis of evidence of student learning to inform and improve its teaching, it will never function as a true collaborative team in a strong PLC. If the purpose of the team is to promote *learning* for students and adults, the issue of how members can use assessment results to improve their own learning must remain at the forefront.

For a useful tool to help teams collaborate effectively and stay focused on the right work, download "Critical Issues for Team Consideration" from www.allthingsplc.info (www.allthingsplc .info/tools-resources/search-result/view/id,96).

Focus on Learning

The emphasis placed on student learning in a virtual collaborative team does not diminish the importance of teaching. In fact, the primary reason to become a member of a virtual collaborative team is to impact and improve teaching. Too often, school reform efforts have swirled around the school but not within the classroom. Schools have changed their schedules, added graduation requirements, administered required tests, and responded to countless other reform initiatives, and yet instructional practice in the classroom tends to remain unchanged. The PLC process is specifically intended to create the conditions to help educators become more skillful in teaching because great teaching and high levels of student learning go hand in hand.

Therefore, the question of what instructional strategies and approaches might help bring more students to higher levels of achievement is implicitly interwoven throughout the entire team process. It is important to note, however, that there is a difference between conversations about how team members *like* to teach a concept or have always taught a concept and examining actual *evidence* of student learning to determine which strategies are most effective. As John Hattie (2009) writes in his expansive study of factors that impact student achievement:

> . . . teaching was carried out largely out of sight and hearing of other teachers, and thus there was a tendency to rely on narrative accounts to construct a shared understanding. So often teachers depended on "war stories," personal experiences, and a reliance on their own experience to justify their personal preferences. If this swapping of war stories is the closest teachers come to professional conversations, the picture is bleak for the messages in this book about teachers needing to share evidence about their teaching with their colleagues. (p. 252)

Furthermore, Richard DuFour and Robert Marzano (2011) write, "Instruction is a means to an end—student learning—and thus the ultimate test of effective instruction is actual evidence that students have learned" (p. 142). Members of a virtual team cannot be content with knowing they taught a concept or covered the material. They cannot be satisfied with knowing that a favorite instructional strategy works for most students. They can't even settle for implementing a new strategy to teach a concept. They must be fixated on the question of whether or not students acquired the intended knowledge and skills. So remember the following takeaway from this chapter: *the potential power of the virtual collaborative process will not be realized until a collaborative team of teachers is jointly examining transparent evidence of student learning and using that evidence to inform and improve the individual and collective instructional practices of its members.*

Time for Collaboration

In its analysis of educational systems around the world, the Organisation for Economic Co-operation and Development (2014a) reports that the "traditional view of teachers as working in a closed classroom in isolation from colleagues still seems to hold true for many U.S. teachers" (p. 1). American teachers spend far more time engaged in large-group, direct instruction per week than their international peers (twenty-seven hours versus nineteen hours). Thus, they have little time to work with colleagues, despite the abundance of research on the benefits of collaborative practice. The report concludes that policymakers in the United States should create structures to support collaboration as part of a teacher's routine work practice. The report also encourages teachers to "seek networking and mentoring opportunities to enhance collaboration" (OECD, 2014a, p. 5).

We fully concur with these conclusions. Too many districts in the United States continue to operate under the assumption that the only time teachers are working is when they are delivering instruction in a classroom. These districts view their school calendars as a dichotomy—teacher "work" days and teacher "learn" days. They assume teachers work (that is, teach) 176 days each year and then learn on the 4 days set aside for professional development. It is time to recognize that in the best schools, teaching and learning are interwoven, enabling teachers to continue to learn as part of their routine work practice. It is also time to realize that educators should be taking greater advantage of the opportunities for networking and mentoring that virtual collaboration affords.

It seems disingenuous for districts to tout their support of teacher collaboration to meet the unique needs of each student and then provide so little time for them to do it. The OECD (2014b) concludes that its study "underscores the need for a new model of teaching. The traditional picture of a single classroom with one teacher in isolation is not good enough for a variety of reasons" (p. 199). We urge districts to recognize the need for this new model, a model that supports educators in building collaborative processes both within their schools and beyond their school walls through virtual collaborative teams.

Conclusion

Many schools and districts operate under the delusion that their educators are operating as members of PLCs because they are assigned to teams and provided with time to collaborate. They are, in a word, wrong. Team structures and time for collaboration are necessary elements of the PLC process, but they are insufficient. Key questions and assumptions must drive the work of teams. Teams must perform certain tasks in their collaborative efforts. If these tasks are not accomplished, even teams with the best of intentions accomplish little. We hope that this chapter helped to clarify the essential work of teams in PLCs.

CHAPTER 7

Virtual Teaming: A Case Scenario

It's easy to get mesmerized by the next best thing. While smartphone technology may continue to amaze, the power of that technology is not in the bells and whistles of the phone but rather in how to use it to become better professionals, parents, friends, and more informed citizens. Strategically designed virtual teams, a commitment to openness, and a thoughtful use of PLNs don't represent a collection of new, compartmentalized gadgets. These structures should enhance the work of all school teams and result in a deeper commitment to the collaborative processes of PLCs at Work. This chapter is devoted to illustrating the application of these concepts in action in a school today—Springfield High School. While Springfield is not a real school, the scenario is modeled after a compilation of schools that have undergone the PLC transformation and used technology to accelerate the work of their teams.

Having worked with multiple schools attempting to use technology more thoughtfully to accelerate collaborative work, we strive to provide some working examples that not only might minimize the mistakes of well-intended leaders but also identify best practice approaches that advance your work in heretofore unrealized ways. Time to get to work!

Springfield High School

Springfield High School is located in the heart of the Midwest and is home to approximately 1,800 students in grades 9–12. There are 112 teachers. Springfield is a blue-collar town that continues to struggle with the changing economy. Over the years, Springfield steadily declined in terms of its performance on statewide tests, and some staff believed that the slide was irreversible. That belief changed, however, when Dr. Gail Stone became principal and subsequently worked with her staff in investigating, adopting, and ultimately fully embracing the PLC process. Like most schools, Springfield struggled at times in its efforts to implement the PLC process. In retrospect, however, it has come a long way in the five years of its PLC journey with substantial progress and improved performance in the most important area of all—student learning.

To the delight of her staff, Gail has a great, self-effacing sense of humor. She makes her new teachers feel particularly welcomed when she comes to them and asks for help in addressing a problem she might be having with a laptop, smartphone, or office PC. Several of her most comfortable teacher colleagues tease Gail about working in the Stone Age when it comes to technology. Gail probably exaggerates her dependence on others for help with technology to promote leadership from the middle, and particularly the leadership of newer teachers—a population of contributors often ignored.

Christine is a mathematics teacher and Mark is a social studies teacher at Springfield High. They have become dear friends and are somewhat of an odd professional couple. Christine is young, liberal, and on the cutting edge of technology utilization. She has a powerful PLN that provides her with meaningful input every day. Mark, three decades her senior and very conservative, shares her penchant for connections through technology, and as a result, they found unexpected common ground. They get along so well that they even invite each other to join various groups within each other's PLNs.

Both Christine and Mark believe in and thoroughly embrace the PLC process but for different reasons. Mark appreciates the purposeful structure for team learning that the process provides. Christine, a natural leader and energetic "doer," loves the action orientation and the sense that she and her teammates are in control of the destiny of their work. When critics of education say, "It can't be done," Christine leads others on her team to say, "Just watch us!"

Christine and Mark are strong advocates for virtual teaming and encouraged Gail to abandon the Stone Age and provide an unequivocal endorsement of the concept. With Gail's support and leadership provided by innovative teachers, like Christine and Mark, the Springfield staff tackled the challenge of utilizing virtual teams as a natural extension of its school-based teams. Following are some examples of the strategies the staff has utilized.

Required Virtual Teaming

Springfield High School has made teaming an integral part of what it does. Although content- and course-specific teams represent the norm at Springfield, the staff utilizes vertical and interdisciplinary team structures as well. To support the implementation of virtual teaming, every team is assigned an asynchronous, parallel meeting place and is expected to use that space to enhance its work.

Several years earlier, Springfield High School teachers began utilizing the school's own local learning management system (LMS) to provide online learning options for their students. In making the transition to virtual teaming, they simply assigned a course-room as a place where team members could connect. While this learning platform works fairly well, teachers soon came to realize there are other interesting options for hosting this virtual teaming space. Springfield decided to make use of the NEA Professional Practice Communities and move its collaborative teams to this learning platform. This particular website has all the advantages of the local LMS, including the capacity to keep its meetings exclusive to invited guests. It also provides an open learning space for the NEA's

3.2 million members and anyone else interested in joining. This allows Springfield's teachers to work within the secure team structure of their school-based PLC while just a few clicks away from other teachers throughout the United States and beyond. The NEA Professional Practice Communities also provide teachers with access to a myriad of posted supports and resources that are expanding every day. Ultimately, this allows Springfield teachers to work in their collaborative teams while simultaneously adding to their own PLNs. It also allows them to open-source various challenges and issues that arise in their school and receive input from educators well beyond Springfield boundaries.

What makes this virtual collaborative meeting space so powerful is that every time Springfield teachers sign in, they are reminded that they are part of a much larger community of educators seeking the most promising practices for meeting students' needs. The simple visibility of all these potential learning partners, along with the still cloistered and intimate collaborative opportunities on each team, makes for a robust learning environment. It also fosters a paradigm shift, recognizing that the teaching profession must foster collaboration and collective efforts rather than individual isolation.

Access to an asynchronous virtual collaborative spaces also helps Springfield teachers who have multiple classes to stay connected with more than one team. Furthermore, as we referenced earlier, the asynchronous learning space allows team members to log on, participate in a virtual threaded conversation, make a contribution, and advance the collective learning forward when it is convenient for them. Colleagues can then reflect on these contributions and respond through the threaded conversations, over lunch, or during their formal team meeting time. Teams are able to avoid the problem of disconnect that can occur when waiting until the next meeting to continue discussion of a topic.

Systemic Commitment to Open Sourcing

Springfield educators did not just plunge into virtual collaboration. With the support of Gail and key teacher leaders, they considered the ten decision points that represent Level 1 engineering of virtual teams. They agreed to honor the strategies for e-collaboration that make up Level 2. Finally, teams also agreed that in order to get to the deepest levels of innovation and take advantage of opportunities that emerge when connecting with others on the outside, it was essential that the culture of Springfield High School remain "open." To that end, every virtual team within the school was expected to adhere to the guidelines for establishing e-acceleration (Level 3) and use open strategies and learning networks to enhance team learning.

Springfield arrived at this decision thanks to a commitment to teacher-led innovation in the school. This cadre of teacher advocates had the wisdom to see that forming these virtual spaces and the power to connect with other professionals represents yet another innovative way to advance their professional practice. The administration had the wisdom to recognize that this represents a level of professionalism and ownership that is altogether necessary in the complex world of school reform today. As a result, building and district administrators are enthusiastically supportive of these efforts.

It's Still About PLCs

Springfield's emphasis on integrating technology into the collaborative team process could have created the false impression that technology is an end unto itself rather than a means to an end. To remind staff that technology is a tool to strengthen its PLC, every year, Gail asks each team to revisit the foundational elements of the PLC process and assess its progress.

The box on page 132 shows an example blog that Gail might post about revisiting the six characteristics of a PLC.

Welcome back! Below, find a list of the six characteristics of a professional learning community. It is our job to work on reinforcing these critical characteristics within each team in our school. In the space just below this list, articulate how well you think your team is doing in terms of implementation, and identify at least two areas in which your team needs to improve, as well as two strengths that you believe your team currently possesses. Once again, you are to reflect on this as a team and the work your team is responsible for.

1. Shared mission (purpose), vision (clear direction), values (collective commitments), and goals (indicators, time lines, and targets), which are all focused on student learning

2. A collaborative culture with a focus on learning

3. Collective inquiry into best practices and current reality

4. Action orientation or "learning by doing"

5. A commitment to continuous improvement

6. Results orientation

Another useful tool to help teams reflect on their practice is the "Professional Learning Communities at Work™ Continuum: Laying the Foundation" in *Learning by Doing* (second edition, DuFour et al., 2010). This continuum asks educators to reflect on each aspect of the PLC process and assess their team's place on a five-point rubric. (Visit **go.solution-tree.com/PLCbooks** to download a copy of the continuum.) Practices like these help reinforce the commitment to sustain the PLC process and the importance of its various elements. Furthermore, by calling for a written response from each team, it encourages reflection and dialogue about the team's PLC journey. The responses help to identify areas of concern or confusion that could be addressed and establish new priorities and goals.

Benefits of Technology for School-Based Teams

As time went on, the Springfield staff discovered some unantici-
pated benefits that resulted from its commitment to use technology
for strengthening and improving its teams. Some of those benefits
include the following.

Consensus at the Team Level

Springfield educators soon discovered that one of the benefits of
asynchronous threaded discussions is the ability to participate in
critical conversations that serve as a precursor to building consensus.
Threaded discussions help Springfield educators become more adept
at resolving conflicts and using differences of opinion to engage in
thoughtful threaded debates. Educators can take time to reflect on
opinions and evidence of best practices before responding. This virtual collaboration platform allows for presentation of ideas, provides
time for thoughtful consideration and responses, encourages inquiry,
and helps teams discover common ground.

Even in well-designed, face-to-face meetings, important observations or information can be overlooked, and the bell can cut discussions short. But with asynchronous threaded conversations, that
same observation or information continues to be accessible to every
member of the team, prompting more thoughtful consideration
and responses. It remains there for others to consider, reread, reflect
on, and react to. When responses are supported by research and
evidence, they help build the shared knowledge that is essential to
creating consensus.

Participation From All Team Members

The collaborative team process in high-performing PLCs requires
each member to contribute to the collective effort, support others,
honor commitments, remain actively engaged, and work interdependently with colleagues to achieve shared goals for which each
member is mutually accountable. Springfield staff soon recognized

that threaded online discussions provide insights regarding the levels of participation among team members. It has become easy to observe the presence (or absence) of each member's contribution to the dialogue. Of course, this indication does not reveal the cause of nonparticipation. Is the team member unclear about the topic, uncertain of how he or she might contribute, reluctant to participate, or overwhelmed with personal or professional issues? Team leaders might discuss the matter with the teacher in an effort to resolve whatever is causing the lack of contribution. What has become evident, however, is that individuals typically take the initiative to engage in the discourse without prompting as it becomes apparent that they are not contributing. The public nature of the threaded conversation encourages participation in ways that face-to-face meetings often do not.

Background Information for New Teachers

For many years, the traditional orientation for new teachers to a school was limited to receiving a copy of the faculty manual, the textbook, and a set of keys to their classrooms. From that point, neophytes were often left to fend for themselves. The collaborative team structure of PLCs is designed to ensure that all new members of the team get the information and support they need to succeed in the classroom. What can be missing, however, is the background story that explains the thought processes the team went through to arrive at its key decisions. New team members can review threaded conversations to gain a better understanding of the context of past decisions and become familiar with past rationale when an issue resurfaces.

Interactive Approach to Faculty Meetings

While Gail continues to have face-to-face faculty meetings, she finds that posting faculty agenda items in an asynchronous learning space better prepares staff for meetings or serves as an alternative to a meeting. Staff members who seek to propose a topic for the agenda are expected to provide a brief written explanation as to why it warrants the staff's attention. They can also provide attachments and links to give background information. The staff can use threaded discussions to ask questions or seek clarification. Although there have been missteps along the way, the general feeling at Springfield is that this structure actually allows for more thoughtful consideration of schoolwide issues.

Deep Cultural Change

In teaching the merits of advanced teaming, virtual collaborative best practices, and the use of open-source acceleration, Casey has had the opportunity to work with a number of corporate clients who are likewise interested in the topic. In almost every instance, he had to sign agreements, promising never to share sacred corporate information with competitors. This is a key differentiator between corporate America and K–12 education, a differentiator that definitely works in our favor. In the case of Casey's corporate clients, sharing powerful innovations with others could result in a lawsuit for him and potentially crippling competitive advantages for the competition. In education, however, there is no such disadvantage, and the opportunities to share innovations and ideas result in better outcomes for everyone.

The Springfield faculty learned to benefit from sharing its collective expertise and using open sourcing to create new knowledge. Springfield teams are learning more, doing more, and developing the individual and collective capacities of their members. As a result, not only has student achievement improved, but the culture of the school also has been so profoundly impacted that it likely will outlast the "Stone Age"—Gail's tenure as principal at Springfield.

Conclusion

The PLC process is designed to ensure participants work together to build shared knowledge—and act on that knowledge—in ways that lead to higher levels of student achievement. The implementation of virtual teams, the utilization of a learning platform with threaded discussions and spaces to catalog information, and the accessibility of internal and external expertise through open sourcing can remove some of the barriers to building that shared knowledge for high levels of learning for all.

CHAPTER 8

Leading School-Based and Virtual Teams

What kind of leadership is most effective in supporting educators as they use technology to create and strengthen both school-based and virtual teams? There is a tendency in the United States to think of leadership as a rare quality that allows extraordinary individuals to use their exceptional charisma and indomitable will to help ordinary people overcome their limitations. According to this image of leadership, a leader is a rare breed possessed of skills far beyond those of the general population. Leaders are the visionary entrepreneurs (Steve Jobs), the brilliant military tacticians (George Patton), and the legendary athletes (Michael Jordan) who single-handedly account for the success of their enterprise. This image of leadership is prevalent in education as well with tales of turnaround principals who save failing schools through their individual efforts.

According to this narrative, leaders don't just have the answer to the problem; they *are* the answer to the problem. This is, once again, classic Taylorism at work. The person at the top of the organizational chart identifies the one best way to solve a problem, and all others do what they are told.

This is not the leadership approach that facilitates the work of educators as they address the challenges of using technology to support collaborative team processes. No one person has all the energy, expertise, or influence to overcome those challenges. The leadership we propose is collective rather than individualistic and is available to people throughout the organization. Furthermore, we reject the autocratic model of leadership and offer the idea of servant leadership instead. We define *servant leadership* as working with others to establish a shared sense of purpose, goals, and direction and then creating the conditions to help them succeed at what they are trying to accomplish. We offer the following six keys to effective servant leadership.

1. Disperse leadership.

2. Establish clarity regarding what needs to be done and why.

3. Monitor and support teams to promote success.

4. Ensure reciprocal accountability.

5. Focus on limited goals and initiatives.

6. Acknowledge and celebrate small wins.

Disperse Leadership

Servant leaders recognize that leadership is not a solo act. Therefore, they purposefully create structures to disperse leadership. They start by creating a guiding coalition or leadership team of influential staff members to help oversee the change initiative. They understand the need to generate support from a small group of advocates before tackling the problem of building widespread consensus with the entire staff. The guiding coalition shares responsibility for building shared knowledge, establishing two-way communication, answering questions and concerns, developing consensus, and steering the PLC process through the inevitable obstacles and setbacks that occur. In other words, these leaders become servant leaders too.

Another structure that supports dispersed leadership is creating the position of team leader for teams that grow beyond a certain number (for example, four members). Team leaders serve as the liaisons between their members and the building leaders. Servant leaders on the guiding coalition are responsible for providing team leaders with the resources, training, and tools to help them lead their teams successfully. Virtual teams are likely to confront unique problems, and while it is not the leadership team's responsibility to have all the answers, it is its responsibility to create the processes that bring the problems to the surface for collective consideration and resolution.

Another opportunity for dispersed leadership in the PLC process is situational leadership based on evidence of effective practice. Consider a team that has worked together to identify the essential outcomes of a unit and developed a common formative assessment to monitor each student's mastery of those outcomes. As the team analyzes the evidence of student learning from its assessment, it becomes apparent that one member has been particularly effective in helping students achieve the intended outcomes. That member would then take the lead in sharing with his or her colleagues the strategy or strategies that proved so effective. In this case, leadership is not based on position or title but on evidence of particular expertise.

Situational leadership certainly comes into play when using technology to enhance building-level teams or to create virtual teams. The technophiles on a team emerge as key leaders in the process based on their expertise with using technology, and other members can lean into them for support.

John Gardner (1990) once argued, "the taking of responsibility is at the heart of leadership. To the extent that leadership tasks are shared, responsibility is shared" (p. 152). Servant leaders don't hoard leadership responsibilities; they disperse them. But they also do more than merely delegate. They provide ongoing feedback and support to help others develop their leadership capacity.

Finally, servant leaders recognize that any improvement effort is unlikely to be sustained for the long term unless they groom others to lead the process when they are no longer there. As Richard DuFour and Michael Fullan (2013) write:

> When an organization has created widespread own-
> ership of the change process and developed the
> leadership potential of its members, people through-
> out the organization take collective responsibility for
> preserving its culture. Positional leaders may come and
> go, but the culture endures because it is grounded in
> collective leadership rather than dependent upon an
> individual. (p. 72)

Put another way, the ultimate test of the servant leader in using technology to strengthen collaborative teams is how many leaders he or she leaves behind who can take the collaborative team process even further.

Establish Clarity Regarding What Needs to Be Done and Why

Rather than dictating what people need to do, servant leaders engage them in building shared knowledge about the reasons why the work must be done. They begin with *why* before *how*. They seek commitment rather than compliance, and they understand that commitment is a by-product of engaging people in the decision-making process.

The assumption driving servant leaders is that if people of good faith have access to the same information when called on to make a decision, they are likely to arrive at similar decisions. So servant leaders set out to ensure that everyone has access to information. They provide research supporting the benefits of creating collaborative teams, provide students with a guaranteed curriculum, monitor student learning on a frequent basis through team-developed common formative assessments, use protocols to analyze evidence of student learning to inform and improve individual and collective practice, and develop systems to ensure students receive additional time and support when they struggle as well as opportunities to extend and enrich learning when they are proficient. They provide training on the PLC process and access to schools that have well-established collaborative teams so staff members can observe the work firsthand.

They may pilot the PLC process with willing course teams or grade levels to identify challenges and benefits before moving to schoolwide implementation. They share information on the power and potential of technology to strengthen and expand collaborative teams. Very importantly, they recognize the need for two-way communication throughout this knowledge-building phase of the process. They rely on conversations more than presentations and dialogue more than monologue so they can hear and respond to questions and concerns that inevitably arise. They appeal to both the head (reasoning) and the heart (emotions). (The website www .allthingsplc.info is an excellent source of research and rationale to support the PLC process, and it includes a list of model PLC schools and districts.)

Servant leaders also recognize that if schools are going to move forward on the PLC journey, at some point, members of the organization must move from *learning* about PLCs and *talking* about PLCs to *doing* what PLCs do. Creating shared knowledge is crucial to their consensus-building process, but there is a difference between consensus and unanimity. As Patrick Lencioni (2005) advises, "Waiting for everyone on a team to agree intellectually on a decision is a good recipe for mediocrity, delay, and frustration" (p. 51). To provide every staff member with veto power over whether or not a school embraces an improvement initiative fosters paralysis, not participation. The better approach to consensus building is this: we have arrived at a consensus when *all* points of view not only have been heard but also solicited and the will of the group becomes evident, even to those who most oppose it. When that benchmark is reached, servant leaders recognize the need for action.

At this juncture, it is critical for leaders to be as specific as possible regarding the concrete steps collaborative teams must take to engage in the process. As Chip and Dan Heath (2010) write:

> If you want people to change, you must provide crystal-clear direction. . . . Many leaders pride themselves on setting high-level direction: *I'll set the vision and stay out of the details.* . . . But it's not enough. Big-picture, hands-off leadership isn't likely to work in a change situation, because the hardest part of change—the paralyzing part—is precisely in the details. . . . Ambiguity is the enemy. Any successful change requires a translation of ambiguous goals into concrete behaviors. (pp. 16, 53–54)

One of the ways in which servant leaders fulfill their responsibility to ensure clarity is to work with staff to establish a few, specific, nondiscretionary aspects of the improvement process that must be honored. One of the stumbling blocks that schools often encounter in the PLC process is determining who decides how teams use their collaborative time—the administration or the teachers. A battle rages over who decides who decides. This is a traditional question of power. In a PLC, the objective, once again, is to make decisions by building shared knowledge—learning together—about the most promising practice. This collective study reveals that there is abundant research establishing that schools are more effective when engaging in the following six nondiscretionary practices.

1. Educators work collaboratively rather than in isolation and have clarified commitments to each other about how they work together.

2. The fundamental structure of the school becomes the collaborative team; members work interdependently to achieve common goals for which all members are mutually accountable.

3. The team establishes a guaranteed curriculum, unit by unit, so all students have access to the same knowledge and skills, regardless of which teacher they are assigned.

4. The team develops common formative assessments to frequently gather evidence of student learning.

5. The school creates systems of intervention to ensure students who struggle receive additional time and support for learning in a way that is timely, directive, diagnostic, and systematic.

6. The team uses evidence of student learning to inform and improve the individual and collective practices of its members.

This list applies to both school-based teams and virtual teams. Anyone exploring the most promising practices for improving student achievement should agree on this list if he or she understands the research behind each practice. (For summaries of the research behind each practice, see *Learning by Doing* [second edition; DuFour et al., 2010].) Therefore, in a PLC, the relevant question isn't about who has the power but, rather, if the team can agree on the most promising practices to benefit students and staff. After reaching that agreement, these aspects of the school culture are considered nondiscretionary, or "tight," and everyone on staff is expected to honor what is tight. The servant leader then becomes responsible for helping to promote and protect these conditions within the school.

Clarity regarding what is tight is just half the equation of an effective school culture. In PLCs, teachers are empowered to make important decisions. For example, consider the previous list of six tight practices of the PLC process. Teams establish their own collective commitments and SMART goals. They have a major voice in deciding the essential elements of the guaranteed curriculum, how to pace the curriculum, the instructional strategies to use, and the assessments to administer. Each team member analyzes the evidence of student learning and contributes to the plans for improving on the individual and collective results of the other members. All these important elements of the PLC process are "loose" in that individuals and teams have the authority to be creative and innovative in their approach to their work, provided they continue to honor what is tight in their school. In short, servant leaders help establish a culture that is simultaneously loose and tight.

Monitor and Support Teams to Promote Success

Leaders often create a false dichotomy when monitoring the work of others. They must choose between micromanaging every detail and laissez-faire leadership, in which they turn people loose and hope for the best. The first strategy fails to create ownership in the process or build the capacity of the staff. The second makes it impossible to support a team that is experiencing difficulty or to learn from a team that is accomplishing great things. Furthermore, one of the important ways that leaders communicate priorities is where they choose to focus their attention. Leaders who are inattentive to the work of teams send the message that the work is unimportant.

Servant leaders can't provide effective support to teams unless they are aware of the obstacles and challenges the teams are facing. One team might lack clarity about the elements of SMART goals. Another team might experience conflict. A third may need help in coordinating schedules to provide time for collaboration. Servant leaders must have a process for monitoring the progress of each team without micromanaging the collaborative team process.

The best solution to this challenge is to work with the guiding coalition and team leaders to establish clarity regarding (1) the products teams generate as a result of the collaborative team process and (2) time lines for when those products are to be completed. Assuming a team is provided with time to meet on a regular basis, the time line for specific products might look like the following.

- After two meetings, present your team's collective commitments.

- After three meetings, present your team's SMART goal.

- After five meetings, present the essential outcomes for the unit your team is about to teach.

- After seven meetings, present your team-developed common formative assessment for the unit.

- After nine meetings, present your team's analysis of student achievement for that unit, your insights as to what worked and what didn't, and your strategies for improving effectiveness in teaching the essential outcomes.

Note that these products represent the natural output of a collaborative team focused on the right work in the PLC process. A collaborative team that is clear on its collective commitments or its essential outcomes should have no difficulty presenting copies of these products to the leadership team. Note also that the time line and products are established collaboratively rather than dictated by the administration.

Ensure Reciprocal Accountability

If servant leaders ask members of their staff to be accountable to the collaborative team process, those leaders also must be accountable by providing teams with everything they need to succeed in what they are being asked to do. This support for the collaborative team process can take many forms. One essential support is providing teams with the time necessary to engage in the work. It is disingenuous for any school or district to espouse the benefits of collaboration and then fail to provide educators with the time to collaborate. To find strategies for providing collaborative time that don't require additional expenditures, go to www.allthingsplc.info /tools-resources/search-result/view/id,77.

Teams also need the appropriate technology and ongoing training in both the PLC process and the best use of technology. This training is most effective if it becomes integrated with the work of the team rather than separate from the work. The best professional development is job embedded, occurring in the workplace rather than in workshops (Elmore, 2004; Fullan, 2005; Fulton & Britton, 2011; Learning Forward, n.d.; Little, 2006).

Beyond providing these fundamental levels of support for teams, servant leaders should stay in ongoing contact with the guiding coalition and team leaders to identify obstacles to progress. For example, one of the largest geographic school districts in the United States included four very small rural high schools. Each school had only one teacher in each subject. The distance between schools made it impossible for teachers to meet in collaborative teams on a regular basis. The schools lacked the technology for virtual meetings, and each school had its own unique schedule, making it impossible to coordinate meetings of subject-area teachers. So although key staff had been trained in the PLC process, the size and structure of the district presented major obstacles to creating a collaborative culture.

Rather than conclude that the team process was impossible in their district, the central office staff, principals, and teacher leaders worked together to identify and overcome obstacles. They made technology available in all four schools that allowed teachers to meet simultaneously in see you–see me meetings. The principals coordinated their school schedules with a common start and end time at each school. They then agreed to establish a common preparation period for each subject area and designated one day each week when teachers could hold their collaborative team meetings. For example, all English teachers would have first period as their designated preparation time and devote every Tuesday to team meetings. Each of the four principals agreed to assume the role of the servant leader for designated teams to support their efforts. This district serves as an excellent example of leaders who define their role as helping to identify and remove obstacles to progress.

Finally, effective leadership of the collaborative team process recognizes that different teams require different levels of support at different times. When a collaborative team is functioning at high levels, the school-based leadership team extends members of that team tremendous autonomy. When a team is struggling due to a lack of clarity or a need for additional expertise or resources, the leadership team provides support and helps to solve the problems.

When a team is dysfunctional due to conflict among members or a lack of commitment to the PLC process, the school-based leadership team becomes more directive and monitors the work of the team more closely. Just as the best teachers use differentiated instruction to meet the varying needs of students, the best school-based leadership teams differentiate the approaches to collaborative teams based on the needs of each team.

Focus on Limited Goals and Initiatives

In all our work with schools and districts, we have never encountered educators who felt that an obstacle to their progress was the lack of a sufficient number of initiatives. No faculties ever told us that they felt if they could just add one more initiative, it would help them create a great school. In too many provinces, states, districts, and individual schools, leadership attention, educator energy, and limited organizational resources are spread too thin over too many activities and initiatives. This constant crush of piling new, disconnected, uncoordinated, fragmented change initiatives onto existing programs is more likely to result in educator confusion, exhaustion, and cynicism than improved student achievement. As Douglas Reeves (2011) writes, "Without focus, even the best leadership ideas will fail, the most ideal research-based initiatives will fail, and the most self-sacrificing earnest leaders will fail. Worst of all, without focus by educational leaders, students and teachers will fail" (p. 14).

Servant leaders do not overwhelm educators with initiatives but instead maintain a laser-like focus on a few key priorities and then stay the course for sustained periods of time. For example, Sanger Unified School District, a high-poverty district in the Central Valley of California, was one of the first in the state to go into program improvement because of consistently poor student achievement. After taking pains to build shared knowledge about the PLC process among staff, district leaders promised they would sustain their commitment to PLCs in order to help their schools improve. Within a few years, the district had exceeded the state's achievement goal, outpaced the state average in each of its schools, and improved its high school graduation rate to 97 percent. The majority of Sanger schools now rank in the top 10 percent in the state when compared to schools with similar demographics (David & Talbert, 2013). Today, Sanger is widely recognized as one of the great turnaround success stories in the United States.

A study of Sanger's incredible improvement attributed the district's success to the following.

- The district maintained a long-term commitment to the PLC process as the framework of its improvement effort. It did not pursue every hot topic or innovation.

- The district avoided a quick-fix mentality and instead created a culture of continuous improvement and a philosophy that the work of improving schools is never done.

- The district demonstrated respect for educators and viewed them as the key to improving student learning. As the study concluded, "Leaders worked to support each teacher team in developing trusting relationships, skills in using common formative assessments, transparency in sharing results and information about their teaching, and mutual accountability for the success of all students" (David & Talbert, 2013, p. 14). In every school, teachers led the grade-level or course-specific teams.

- Changes in leadership have not led to changes in direction. The district adopted a "grow-their-own" approach to leadership, believing that those familiar with the Sanger culture and practices would be best equipped to preserve them. Since 2008, not one principal or central office leader has been brought into the district from the outside. Even though the central office leadership that began the initiative has retired (including Marc Johnson, who was named the national superintendent of the year in 2011), the process continues to improve under newly appointed leaders from within (David & Talbert, 2013).

The most effective leaders recognize that having teams implement technology to improve the collaborative process is a significant undertaking requiring sustained support over a long period of time. They not only attempt to buffer those teams from new initiatives but also seek ways to remove high-time, low-leverage tasks from their plates to help focus on the challenge at hand. For example, Ed Rafferty, the Illinois Superintendent of the Year in 2012, surveyed principals and teacher leaders to create a list of "stop doing" tasks required by the central office that contributed little to school improvement and took away time that educators could use to focus on the PLC process. For example, when he discovered that the district's requirement for presenting extensive school improvement plans was cumbersome and time consuming, educators worked together to streamline the process.

Acknowledge and Celebrate Small Wins

In *Cultures Built to Last*, DuFour and Fullan (2013) write:

> Commitment to continuous improvement is vital to deep cultural change, but it can also degenerate into an endless cycle of setting ever-higher goals and taking a never-ending series of steps toward a constantly moving target. The constant push for better results can easily turn into drudgery. It is imperative, therefore, that a culture of continuous improvement be balanced by a culture committed to the identification and celebration of small wins all along the journey. Incremental progress must be noted and honored, not only at the start of an improvement effort, but throughout that effort as well. (p. 61)

The most consistent finding of those who have examined the question of how systems and organizations sustain continuous improvement comes down to this: proactively create, identify, and celebrate small wins. Servant leaders don't just hope for small wins; they plan for small wins. They look for benchmark moments when all teams have completed a task or a particular team has overcome an obstacle, and they intentionally create forums to share those accomplishments with the entire staff. A longitudinal study of what employees value most reveals their need to feel appreciated (Kouzes & Posner, 2003). Most organizations, however, and certainly most schools "astonishingly [under-communicate] the genuinely positive, appreciative, and admiring experiences of [their] members" (Kegan & Lahey, 2001, p. 92).

Following are several keys to effective recognition and celebration of small wins.

- **Be sure that recognition and celebration are "now that," not "if then."** Daniel Pink's (2009) research establishes the idea that external rewards are counterproductive when it comes to energizing knowledge workers like educators. A reward based on the premise "*If* you accomplish this goal, *then* I will recognize you" is an external reward. Servant leaders focus instead on "now that" recognition, such as "*Now that* I have discovered this wonderful accomplishment of one of our teams, I want to share it with the rest of you."

- **Explicitly link recognition and celebration to the mission, vision, collective commitments, and goals of the school.** Staff members should be reminded that the purpose of the celebration is to reinforce what the staff values and to sustain the improvement effort. Celebration is a powerful tool for reminding people about what is important in the school or district.

- **Make recognition and celebration everyone's responsibility.** The servant leader may initially need to model the commitment to celebrating small wins, but ultimately, this responsibility should be shared among the entire staff. Anyone who observes a colleague or colleagues engaging in work he or she truly admires and appreciates should be encouraged to share this admiration with the staff. Time should be specifically set aside to allow for this recognition.

- **Do not limit recognition and celebration to monumental accomplishments.** The key to creating a celebratory culture is not waiting for monumental achievements but focusing instead on small wins. Big challenges should be broken down into incremental tasks, and completion of those tasks should be celebrated. When every team establishes its collective commitments, celebrate! When every team writes a common formative assessment, celebrate! Rather than waiting for major milestones, celebrate "inch pebbles." As the Heath brothers (2010) write, "When you engineer early successes, what you're really doing is engineering hope" (p. 7). When you set small, visible goals and people achieve them, they get it into their heads that they can succeed.

- **Avoid major prizes as a form of celebration.** Frequent public acknowledgments for a job well done and a wide distribution of small, symbolic gestures of appreciation and admiration are far more powerful tools for communicating priorities than infrequent "grand prizes" that create a few winners and many losers. Effective celebration convinces every member of the staff that he or she can be a winner and that his or her efforts can be acknowledged and appreciated.

One of the most frequent concerns expressed by educators who are wary of making celebration a part of their school or district is that if celebration is frequent, it loses its impact. Yet research draws the opposite conclusion; it reaffirms that frequent celebration communicates priorities, connects people to the organization and to each other, and sustains improvement initiatives (Amabile & Kramer, 2011; Heath & Heath, 2010; Patterson, Grenny, Maxfield, McMillan, & Switzler, 2008).

Can celebration be overdone? Absolutely. The criterion for assessing the appropriateness of recognition for a team or individual should be the sincerity with which recognition is given. Commendation should represent genuine and heartfelt appreciation and admiration. If sincerity is lacking, celebration can be counterproductive.

Conclusion

There is a certain irony when it comes to effective servant leadership in building the capacity of educators to use technology for enhancing their collaborative teams. At the outset of the process, leaders play a vital role in dispersing leadership, providing clarity, monitoring and supporting teams, limiting initiatives, and acknowledging and celebrating small wins. They must be deeply engaged in the process. As virtual teams become more comfortable and familiar with the nature of their work and demonstrate their ability to engage in the work at a high level, they become more self-directed. Servant leaders then become less essential. But that is the essence of servant leadership—helping others to become more autonomous and to recognize and believe in their individual and collective abilities to accomplish greatness.

CHAPTER 9

Reaching the Tipping Point

In September 2014, Rick visited his internist in Lynchburg, Virginia, due to a chronic cough. The doctor ordered a chest X-ray that revealed nodules on his right lung. Unsure as to the meaning of the results, the doctor ordered a CT scan to gather more information. Much to everyone's surprise, the scan revealed that the lower lobe of Rick's right lung had collapsed. The doctor was uncertain as to the cause of the collapse and referred Rick to a pulmonologist for further examination. The pulmonologist conducted a bronchoscopy, a procedure used to investigate airways and examine the lungs. She took small samples of tissue from his lungs, examined them, and assured him after the procedure that nothing seemed out of the ordinary. To be certain, however, she sent samples of the tissue to a pathologist for a more thorough analysis. The pathologist was puzzled by what he saw and uncertain how to interpret it. He contacted a leading authority at the Mayo Clinic in Rochester, Minnesota, for assistance in reading the results. The pathologist at the Mayo Clinic advised everyone concerned that Rick was suffering from adenocarcinoma, the most common form of non-small-cell lung cancer.

After a series of CT scans and PET scans, doctors recommended that Rick undergo surgery to remove the tumor that had crushed the lower lobe of his right lung. According to Rick's research, the leading lung cancer center was Memorial Sloan Kettering in New York City,

so he made arrangements to have the surgery there. During the oper-
ation, however, the surgeon discovered that the cancer had spread
to the other two lobes of the lung, and so the surgery was aborted.

At that point, the surgeon referred Rick to an oncologist at Sloan
Kettering, who laid out a plan for chemotherapy treatment. Rick
asked if the treatments could be coordinated with and conducted
by an oncologist in Lynchburg. The Sloan Kettering doctor readily agreed, and for the next four months, the two doctors—one in
New York and one in Virginia—engaged in a collaborative effort to
administer and monitor Rick's treatments.

As the treatments came to an end and decisions had to be made
about the next steps, Rick opted to participate in a clinical trial at
the University of Virginia. Three different oncologists in New York
and Virginia were working together in a collaborative effort to identify the best strategies for meeting Rick's needs.

The Moral of the Story

There are several elements to this story that warrant attention.
First, none of the doctors relied solely on his or her experience,
expectations, or predictions in analyzing the problem. The internist did not hear any indication of lung problems during the examination. Furthermore, Rick was very physically active and was not
having difficulty with shortness of breath. The internist's experience
and the laws of probability did not suggest a lung problem, but
to be certain, he called for the X-ray. The fact that Rick had never
smoked and had no history of any form of cancer on either side of
his family suggested to the pulmonologist that cancer was not the
cause of his collapsed lung. To be sure, however, she conducted the
bronchoscopy. She saw no evidence of anything abnormal during
the procedure, but to be sure, she sent tissue samples to pathology.
The pathologist was uncertain about Rick's diagnosis, but to be sure,
he reached out to an expert at the Mayo Clinic. The CT scan and
PET scan showed no indication of the spread of cancer beyond the

lower lobe of the right lung, but to be sure, the surgeon sent tissue samples of the middle and upper lobes to pathology and waited to proceed with the surgery until he received word on if the cancer had spread. In each instance, the professional expanded his or her assessment to seek help from others to confirm or disprove his or her initial conclusions.

What is even more noteworthy, however, is that these professionals were so comfortable in soliciting the assistance of others. There was no shame in calling on a specialist or those renowned for expertise in a particular field. The decision to seek help or consult with others was not viewed by anyone as somehow diminishing a particular doctor. In fact, there was an expectation that in order to best meet the needs of patients seeking their services, these professionals would naturally tap into the expertise of those beyond their office, their hospital, or their state. To fail to do so would have been considered profoundly unprofessional.

Rick's situation is not unique. The medical field has embraced the idea that quality care requires collaboration and a collective effort. A comprehensive study of one of the most highly regarded healthcare systems in the United States, the Mayo Clinic, concludes that two core values drive the work of everyone within the system: "The needs of the patient come first," and "[m]edicine should be practiced as a cooperative science" (Berry & Seltman, 2008, p. 65). The authors report, "Collaboration, cooperation, and coordination are the three dynamics that support the practice of team medicine at Mayo Clinic" (Berry & Seltman, 2008, p. 65) where "teamwork is not optional: it is mandatory" (Berry & Seltman, 2008, p. 51). In recounting the system's history, the Mayo Clinic website reports that the founders of the clinic, Dr. William Worrall Mayo and his sons, Will and Charlie, operated from the premise that "[n]o one is big enough to be independent of others" and that the combined wisdom of one's peers was greater than any individual's (Mayo Clinic, 2014, p. 6). The teamwork approach generates continuous staff interactions through which physicians teach each other and support each other's growth. That tradition of collaboration continues today within and among the Mayo Clinic (2014) sites in Minnesota, Arizona, and Florida.

We are not suggesting that the fields of medicine and education are identical. There are significant differences between the two. We are suggesting, however, that it would be naïve, if not arrogant, for educators to assume their world is so unique that they cannot learn from and apply the best practices of those outside of education. Certainly, the propositions that "the needs of the student come first" and "education should be practiced as a cooperative endeavor" warrant consideration. Certainly, the combined wisdom of one's peers offers greater insights into the most promising practices than the views of a single individual. Certainly, students and educators alike can benefit from a teamwork approach in which teachers and principals teach each other, share their insights, and take a continuous interest in each other's growth.

Changing the Traditional Culture

Unlike staff at the Mayo Clinic, educators must overcome one disadvantage in establishing a collaborative culture: the origins of their institutions fostered a tradition of isolation rather than one of collaboration and collective effort. As the United States grew larger, the original one-room schoolhouse simply became a collection of one-room schoolhouses combined under a single roof. Within the same school, the content of the curriculum, the amount of time devoted to particular skills or concepts, the ways in which students were assessed, the factors that went into determining their grades, the frequency with which their parents were kept informed of their achievement, and countless other factors varied widely from classroom to classroom, depending on the practices of individual teachers. The structure and culture of schooling reinforced the message that "When I close my door, I am the king or queen of my kingdom. These are *my* kids, and I don't need anyone interfering in how I deal with *my* kids." For more than four decades, researchers have cited this tradition of educator isolation as a major barrier to substantive school improvement.

Fortunately, the culture of schooling is changing to support the idea of ongoing professional collaboration, a collective approach to meeting the needs of students, evidence-based decision making, and the importance of tapping into the expertise of others to promote continuous improvement. The best school systems around the world are focusing on removing the walls of educator isolation and helping teachers and principals become skilled in the PLC process. We hope that movement in this direction accelerates. But, as we stated earlier, if educators change the fundamental structure of their schools from isolated teachers to isolated teams, the potential of the PLC process to improve adult and student learning will significantly and unnecessarily diminish. It is time for our profession to expand its horizons beyond the classroom, beyond the team, beyond the school, and beyond the district to access the collective expertise available to its members.

Reaching the Tipping Point

As mentioned in the introduction, the "tipping point" is the magic moment when an idea, trend, or social behavior crosses a threshold and spreads like an epidemic (Gladwell, 2002). We are hopeful that our profession is approaching the tipping point at which educators readily access the expertise of colleagues both within their teams and schools and beyond. The conditions that fuel our hope include the following.

Recognize the Potential of the PLC Process

As we established in the introduction, researchers, professional organizations, and practitioners have increasingly regarded the PLC process as the best hope for substantive school improvement. We may be approaching the point described by Mike Schmoker (2004), "when the absence of a 'strong professional learning community' in a school is an embarrassment" (p. 431).

Grow Consensus for Teaching Essential Skills

We may be arriving at a point in time when there is general agreement regarding essential skills for students and the best way to ensure students acquire those skills. In 2002, a coalition of the business community, policymakers, and education leaders (including the NEA) created the Partnership for 21st Century Schools to clarify the knowledge and skills students needed for the new century. The Partnership agreed schools must prepare students to collaborate and cooperate as members of diverse teams, assume shared responsibility for collaborative work, and demonstrate a commitment to learning as a lifelong process. The Partnership recognized that these skills are best learned in a culture that models them for students. Therefore, it called for schools to function as "professional learning communities that enable educators to collaborate, share best practices, and integrate 21st century skills into classroom practice" (Partnership for 21st Century Skills, n.d.a). The Partnership also called for professional development that "encourages knowledge sharing among communities of practitioners, using face-to-face, virtual, and blended communications" (Partnership for 21st Century Skills, n.d.a).

Provide Educators With Time to Collaborate

Providing time for teachers to collaborate is becoming the norm in American education. That time needs to be greatly expanded, but there is growing recognition that providing time for collaboration can advance both adult and student learning.

Establish a New Approach to Assessment

One of the more promising transformations occurring in the education profession is the use of assessment. Traditionally, assessment was regarded as a tool to provide students with an opportunity to prove what they learned and teachers with a basis for assigning a grade. Today, there is growing recognition that assessment can and should be used as a tool to further both student and adult learning. Daily checks for student understanding in the classroom and the periodic gathering of evidence of student learning through team-developed common formative assessments are now being used to help teachers make decisions about where to go next with instruction, help students identify their learning needs, and inform and improve the individual and collective practices of collaborative teaching teams.

Recognize the Disconnect Between Mission and Tradition

Read mission statements from schools and districts throughout North America, and almost all of them are based on the premise that "all students must learn." We believe most educators are sincere when they develop these statements, and they would prefer that all their students did, in fact, learn. Ask those same educators whether they believe that if *all* students must learn, then some students need more time and support than others. Almost certainly, they would agree. But if you then ask if their schools have a systematic process to guarantee that any student who struggles to understand a skill or concept receives additional time and support for learning that goes beyond what the classroom teacher can provide, until recently, the answer would be, "No." Another of the promising developments in education is the growing recognition that when students are not learning, the school must have a systematic plan for providing them with extra time and support rather than leaving the issue for each teacher to decide on individually. Schools might grapple with the challenge of how to best provide interventions, but at least they are addressing an issue that has been too often ignored in the past.

Integrate the Power of Ubiquitous Technology

As we established throughout this book, the power and pervasiveness of technology have made access to expertise more available than at any time in American history. Educators now have the means to expand their collaboration and collective inquiry far beyond the walls of their schools.

Utilize Technologically Savvy Professionals

To the baby boomers who staffed our schools in the final quarter of the 20th century, efforts to integrate new technology into the teaching and learning process represented a revolution. But the new generation of educators entering the profession today has been using technology since infancy. No revolution is required for them. Using technology to enhance their professional practice simply replicates how they use technology to improve their personal lives.

If members of our profession make a sincere commitment to utilizing the potential and power of technology to strengthen their collaborative teams, expanding their access to expertise, and widening the net of their collective inquiry, the tipping point for education may be within reach.

A Final Word

A professional is someone who requires both (1) extensive training in using a complex body of knowledge and skills in order to enter the field and (2) ongoing training to maintain and expand on that body of knowledge and skills. It is not uncommon for a doctor to say, "I have been practicing medicine for twenty years," or for a lawyer to announce, "I have been practicing law for fifteen years." But when educators state they have been "practicing teaching," they typically refer to that part of their college experience when they are expected to learn everything there is to know about teaching.

It is time for members of our profession to assert proudly, "I have been practicing the art and science of teaching for twenty years." In order to do so, we must create the conditions for ongoing professional learning and development that occur not merely in workshops or graduate courses but as contributing members of a collaborative effort to identify and solve the incredibly complex challenges educators confront today.

We must become more comfortable with soliciting the assistance of others. We must recognize that there is no shame in calling on someone with greater expertise. We must acknowledge that in order to best meet the needs of students seeking our professional services, we must naturally tap into the wisdom of those beyond our classroom, our school, or our state. To fail to do so is profoundly unprofessional.

The time for this transformation is now.

Appendix:
Reproducibles

Four Examples of Organizing Virtual Teams

Example 1: Adding Virtual Teams to a Traditional PLC

The Scenario: Lincoln Middle School has been implementing the PLC process for five years. The staff decide that they want to take whatever steps necessary to accelerate their progress. As a result, they are going to get serious about implementing virtual teams in their PLC team structure to improve communication and collaboration.

Membership	Closed: Only members of the current grade level or content area teams are formal, ongoing members of the virtual team.
Connection	Hybrid (virtual / face to face): Teams obviously continue to meet face to face but also use virtual teaming to enhance the learning.
Scope	Team: While the school plans to utilize virtual teaming in a number of creative ways, staff members are steadfastly committed to making sure that every team in their PLC is accelerated with a structured virtual team.
Format	Hybrid (asynchronous/synchronous): Since virtual teaming doesn't take the place of traditional, face-to-face, synchronous meetings, the asynchronous aspects of the teams provide an opportunity for ongoing dialogue, reflection, and growth.
Orientation	Grade level / content area: Every grade level or content area in the school that currently has a PLC team forms a virtual team to serve as a companion to ongoing efforts.

page 1 of 8

Duration	Ongoing: Commitment to the PLC model requires ongoing commitment to teaming. In this case, there is an ongoing commitment to using virtual teaming to support that process.
Origin	Planned: The school makes a planned, strategic commitment to using virtual teams to improve and accelerate the performance of traditional teams within the PLC.
Purpose	Learn and transform: As is the purpose of every team within a PLC, the virtual team serves to accelerate the learning and continuous transformation of professional practice and improvement of outcomes.
Size	Limited: Teams are limited only to the assigned members.
Management	Facilitative: The school uses the same organization style for traditional teams as it does for virtual teams. Its efforts are one and the same, with the technology and strategies of virtual teams simply accelerating the progress.

Example 2: Supporting At-Risk Latino Middle School Students

The Scenario: Hope Spring Middle School has experienced a massive influx of English learners (ELs) in the last five years. Most of these students are Spanish speaking. Recently, several critical incidents have occurred involving students running away and being suspended. There is also a trend of low performance on long-standing local assessments. Virtual teaming is being used in response to these issues.

Membership	Closed: Since this team is anticipating some rather intense discussions with a focused group of educators, team members decide to make it a closed group.
Connection	Hybrid (virtual / face to face): The group connection is primarily virtual with some face-to-face opportunities throughout the year.
Scope	Regional: Teachers from this school choose to include educators from throughout their region as members of this virtual team. This is because many other schools in the area are also experiencing this new challenge.
Format	Hybrid (asynchronous/synchronous): Since they plan on meeting several times throughout the year yet maintain virtual collaborative space, they define their format as a hybrid.
Orientation	Function: This is a special project outside the traditional work of teams within a middle school PLC.
Duration	Term: This team intends to complete its analysis by the end of the school year.

PLCs at Work™ and Virtual Collaboration: On the Tipping Point of Transformation
© 2016 Solution Tree Press • solution-tree.com • Visit **go.solution-tree.com/PLCbooks** to download this page.

Origin	Unplanned: In the middle of the school year, a group of teachers began reflecting on the need to gather more critical information on supporting the needs of at-risk Latino middle school students.
Purpose	Ignite/inform: This team is determined to improve its service to these students. Team members know, however, that they must develop new knowledge and understanding in order to do so.
Size	Limited: They decide to limit the team to between fifteen and twenty educators.
Management	Facilitative: Although participants come from throughout the region, many of them already know one another, and a facilitative style will likely elicit the most creative thoughts and expressions.

PLCs at Work™ and Virtual Collaboration: On the Tipping Point of Transformation

Example 3: Implementing New State Science Standards

The Scenario: New state science standards recently have been introduced. The standards document is quite voluminous, and there is much to learn about what the standards mean for issues of local curriculum alignment and instruction. As a result, Strongville High School forms a virtual team to examine the issue.

Membership	Open: This core team of science educators commits to meeting consistently and posting as much new information as possible about the new science standards. However, the educators decide not to limit membership and instead allow any other science educators who would like to join the group to participate during their six-month analysis.
Connection	Virtual: Most of this team's work takes place on virtual platforms. However, there may be face-to-face opportunities that follow.
Scope	Regional/state: This initiative prompts team members to identify colleagues from across the state who likewise will be dealing with these issues. The advantage is that connections can be made and resources shared.
Format	Asynchronous: Because most participants never attend a meeting but participate by posting responses and information online, the asynchronous design serves the intentions of this team most efficiently.
Orientation	Function: This team is designed to examine a specific issue outside the normal working parameters of teamwork in a PLC.

Duration	Term: The team elects to limit its work to six months, resulting in a report to be sent to the state legislature and department of education.
Origin	Planned: A team of interested science teachers from across the state decides to put together a virtual team to study the new standards.
Purpose	Ignite/inform, learn and transform, and give voice / send a message: This team intends to learn as much as it can about the new science standards (ignite / inform). The team members also hope that their efforts will inform the work of science teachers everywhere across the state (send a message). They ultimately hope this leads to better practices for every science department in schools throughout the state (learn and transform).
Size	Unlimited: In this case, it's an open membership designed to identify a maximum number of solutions and begin to collate responses to the new state science standards. Allowing the team to grow to an unlimited number (at least for a while) offers the team the opportunity to gather the most amount of information.
Management	Minimal: Since participation is wide open, creative, and seeking unsolicited responses, a minimal managerial approach most likely allows for the greatest amount of participation.

PLCs at Work™ and Virtual Collaboration: On the Tipping Point of Transformation

Example 4: Forming a Vertical Team Within a PLC

The Scenario: Recently, new state mathematics standards have been developed. In response, districts from around the state are concerned that this may require significant curriculum realignment. The Green Plains School District decides to form a local district vertical team to study the issue for one year.

Membership	Closed: This vertical team is focused on a specific set of pre-established learning objectives. As a result, a closed, dedicated team is advantageous.
Connection	Hybrid (virtual / face to face): The district has a learning management system (LMS) that is appropriate for virtual teaming. It keeps notes and maintains threaded dialogue.
Scope	Local district: Because the vertical team involves teachers from a variety of grade levels, district participation is required.
Format	Hybrid (asynchronous/synchronous): The team agrees to meet consistently face to face followed by ongoing dialogue and sharing asynchronously on a virtual platform.
Orientation	Function: In this case, the special function is the vertical examination of essential grade-level or content issues by a team within a PLC.
Duration	Term (one year): This virtual team meets for one year to study this specific issue. Other vertical teams within a PLC may represent an ongoing commitment.

PLCs at Work™ and Virtual Collaboration: On the Tipping Point of Transformation

Origin	Planned: Vertical teams are very common within PLCs. Assuming that a vertical team has existed for years in a district, a virtual team could be a companion to this work to expand its outcomes.
Purpose	Learn and transform: Pursuant to the ongoing purposes of a traditional PLC, the purpose is to learn and transform.
Size	Limited: This team consists of fifteen members across grades K–12.
Management	Facilitative: The team executes this special vertical function pursuant to the ongoing norms and expectations of teams within a PLC.

PLCs at Work™ and Virtual Collaboration: On the Tipping Point of Transformation

Websites to Support Virtual Collaboration

This list of websites could be useful to your collaborative teams as you search for resources to inform and improve your individual and collective instructional practice.

https://learnzillion.com: This site provides brief videos of master teachers presenting key concepts and skills in mathematics and language arts. It also includes resources and "coaches commentary" videos that explore how the lessons are presented.

http://betterlesson.com: This site provides more than five thousand lessons for the Common Core created by master teachers. The site also includes downloadable resources for each lesson.

www.khanacademy.org: The Khan Academy was created to provide students with access to self-directed learning. It provides more than six thousand video tutorial lessons in mathematics, science, history, and more. The site also offers free resources and assessments.

www.teachingchannel.org: The Teaching Channel offers videos of lessons and related materials in most subject areas and grade levels.

www.learner.org/resources/series32.html: The Annenberg Learner site offers video lessons of mathematics concepts for grades K–12.

http://mathflix.luc.edu: Sponsored by Loyola University and Chicago Gear Up Alliance, this site offers more than one thousand video lessons organized by the National Council of Teachers of Mathematics (NCTM) mathematics standards.

www.readwritethink.org: Sponsored by the National Council of Teachers of English (NCTE), this site offers lessons, web resources, student materials, and literacy engagement for K–12 language arts.

Glossary of Terms

A

Action research: A process of collective inquiry in which individuals work together to become more proficient at identifying and solving problems. The steps of action research include (1) formulating a problem, (2) identifying and implementing a strategy to address the problem, (3) creating a process for gathering evidence of the effectiveness of the strategy, (4) collecting and analyzing the evidence, and (4) making decisions based on the evidence.

Asynchronous learning and communication: A process that transfers knowledge and ideas among individuals or groups without the barriers of time and space. Participants can access conversations and lessons at their own pace and according to their own schedules, allowing for the appropriate think time and reflection periods.

C

Capacity building (individual/collective): "Developing the collective ability—dispositions, skills, knowledge, motivation, and resources—to act together to bring about positive change" (Fullan, 2005, p. 4).

Coblabberation: The antithesis of thoughtful collaboration, this is when teams get together and fail to follow protocol and use team time for "blabbing" instead of collaborating.

Collaboration: A systematic process in which people work together, interdependently, to analyze and impact professional practice in order to improve individual and collective results. In a PLC, collaboration focuses on the critical questions of learning: *What is it we want our students to know and be able to do? How will we know if our students are learning? How will*

PLCs at Work™ and Virtual Collaboration: On the Tipping Point of Transformation
© 2016 Solution Tree Press • solution-tree.com • Visit **go.solution-tree.com/PLCbooks** to download this page.

we respond when students do not learn? How will we enrich and extend the learning for students who are proficient?

Collaborative culture: The ongoing process of creating a school culture in which collaboration is at the heart of ongoing efforts in a school to communicate, learn, grow, and evolve.

Collective commitments: The third pillar of the PLC foundation. Collective commitments (or values) represent the promises made among and between all stakeholders that answer the question, What must we do to become the organization we agreed we hope to become?

Collective inquiry: The process of building shared knowledge by clarifying the critical questions that a group explores together. In PLCs, educators engage in collective inquiry to investigate effective practices, examining both external evidence (such as research) and internal evidence (teachers who are getting the best results). They also build shared knowledge regarding the reality of the current practices and conditions in their schools or districts.

Common assessment: An assessment of student learning that uses the same instrument, or a common process utilizing the same criteria, for determining the quality of student work. State and provincial assessments and district benchmark assessments are "common" assessments. However, in a PLC, teams of teachers also create common assessments, assuming collective responsibility for the learning of a group of students who are expected to acquire the same knowledge and skills. Team-developed common assessments provide teachers with the basis of comparison that turns data into information and helps individuals identify strengths and weaknesses in their instructional strategies. They also help identify problem areas in the curriculum that require attention.

Consensus building: Consensus is achieved when (1) all points of view not only have been heard but also have been solicited

PLCs at Work™ and Virtual Collaboration: On the Tipping Point of Transformation
© 2016 Solution Tree Press • solution-tree.com • Visit **go.solution-tree.com/PLCbooks** to download this page.

and (2) the will of the group is evident even to those who most oppose it.

Continuous improvement process: The ongoing cycle of planning, doing, checking, and acting designed to improve results—constantly. In a PLC, this cycle includes gathering evidence of current levels of student learning, developing strategies and ideas to build on strengths and address weaknesses in that learning, implementing those strategies and ideas, analyzing the impact of the changes to discover what was effective and what was not, and applying new knowledge in the next cycle of continuous improvement.

Critical conversations: While even casual conversations within a PLC can help teams realize broader objectives, critical conversations challenge team members to reconsider their assumptions and make their own professional practice open to examination and thoughtful reflection by other members.

D

Dialogue: The sustained collective inquiry into everyday experience and what we take for granted. It makes people "more aware of the context around their experience, and of the processes of thought and feeling that created that experience" (Senge, Kleiner, Roberts, Ross, & Smith, 1994, p. 353). Dialogue is "the capacity to discuss the undiscussable" (Kanter, 2004, p. 81).

Dispersed leadership: A type of servant leadership that recognizes the need for and benefits of developing leaders throughout an organization.

E

e-Acceleration: In this text, e-acceleration refers to the steps educators can take to accelerate learning and innovation opportunities for the team or for a broader audience by utilizing connectivity tools to reach beyond local school boundaries to discover, generate, and apply new ideas and solutions.

e-Collaboration: The steps educators can take to follow accepted strategies, roles, and protocols in relation to learning and interacting in virtual learning spaces. E-collaboration also refers to the steps educators can take to maximize collaborative opportunities with appropriate strategies related to virtual collaboration.

e-Connection: This book references the term *e-connection* in relation to planning activities in which educators participate to develop team objectives and interactions expected as a result of the work of virtual teams. Investment in e-connection or the planning process helps team members make appropriate design choices to put the team in a better position to yield the best possible outcomes.

Engagement: Learning phraseology related to the degree of individual or team neurological energy devoted to a particular learning experience or task. Highly engaged learners bring a stimulated brain to the learning or innovation experience. The degree to which a team within a PLC is engaged drives team members' levels of learning, the development of shared knowledge, and their ability to innovate.

Enrichment: The process of offering alternative learning experiences for students who have met standards. It is a mistake to confuse enrichment with extra work. Assigning an advanced student extra problems isn't enrichment. Enrichment, in many cases, involves the establishment of an entirely different set of learning experiences.

Evidence of student learning: Because learning is the ultimate goal of a PLC, teams within a PLC are consistently striving for increasingly valid measures of student learning, as represented by some measure of quantifiable evidence. Evidence can come in the form of locally developed test scores, qualitative narrative notes, and other agreed-on evidentiary standards that demonstrate the level of student learning attained.

Expertise/competence: This term refers to striving, on a continuous basis, to accelerate what's possible in terms of improving student learning and a focus on developing certain skills, competencies, or professional abilities that ultimately contribute to these new outcomes for students.

G

Guaranteed and viable curriculum: This refers to a curriculum that (1) gives students access to the same essential learning, regardless of who is teaching the class and (2) can be taught in the time allotted (Marzano, 2003).

Guiding coalition: An alliance of key members of an organization who are specifically charged with leading a change process through the predictable turmoil. Members of the coalition should have shared objectives and high levels of trust.

H

Horizontal teaming: Team structures that include educators who are teaching the same course or who serve students in the same grade level. Fourth-grade teachers or all teachers teaching eighth-grade science are examples of horizontal teaming.

I

Innovation: The establishment, promotion, and implementation of novel strategies and approaches. Change happens randomly with the passage of time. Innovation is strategic, deliberate, and designed to produce improved or enhanced results.

Interdisciplinary teams: These teams are made up of educators serving students from multiple disciplines.

PLCs at Work™ and Virtual Collaboration: On the Tipping Point of Transformation

Isolation: The antithesis of teaming and connectivity. Teachers who are not an active part of a PLC may feel they are on their own as they attempt to solve the complex myriad of challenges inherent in meeting the needs of large numbers of students.

L

Laissez-faire leadership: A leadership style wherein the members of an organization have complete control and freedom to make decisions. Leaders are "hands-off" and give autonomy to the members of the organization. In other words, leaders turn people loose and hope for the best.

Learning (individual/collective): The acquisition of new knowledge or skills through ongoing action and perpetual curiosity. Members of a PLC engage in the ongoing study and constant reflective practice that characterize an organization committed to continuous improvement.

Learning targets: At their most granular level, teams within a PLC identify specific learning targets that they expect each student to reach in all units of study they design and teach. These learning targets are then consistently measured, and instructional practice is evaluated against the relative ascent of student progress toward these targets.

M

Micromanaging: A leadership style wherein a leader controls and monitors every detail of a project or situation. Team members are given no freedom or autonomy because the leader watches every move they make.

Millennials: The generation in the early 1980s through the early 2000s that often possesses traits such as the following: is confident about the future, is team oriented, feels pressure to achieve in his or her education and professional life, and is comfortably reliant on technology.

Mission (purpose): The fundamental purpose of an organization. Mission answers the question, Why do we exist?

Mutual accountability: The commitment that team members can count on one another to fulfill their commitments and contribute to the success of the team.

O

Openness: The philosophy of enhancing individual and team learning by utilizing technology to reach out beyond local boundaries; challenge old paradigms; and transform how teams think, learn, and innovate.

Open source: A term referring to strategies that reach beyond the team or school level. In larger districts, a team may elect to apply open-source approaches to other schools in its district. More commonly, however, the scope of open-source strategies would be either regional/state or national/international.

P

Professional: Someone with expertise in a specialized field; an individual who not only has pursued advanced training to enter the field but also is expected to remain current in its evolving knowledge base.

Professional learning community (PLC): An ongoing process in which educators work collaboratively in recurring cycles of collective inquiry and action research to achieve better results for the students they serve. PLCs operate under the assumption that the key to improved learning for students is continuous job-embedded learning for educators.

Proficiency: An agreed-on level of performance wherein competence is established at a level deemed acceptable by a team. Maintaining agreed-on levels of proficiency regarding identified learning objectives helps to minimize confusion and maximize planning opportunities for teams en route to improving professional practice.

R

Reciprocal accountability: The premise that leaders who call on members of the organization to engage in new work, achieve new standards, and accomplish new goals have a responsibility to those members to develop their capacity to be successful in meeting these challenges: "For every increment of performance we ask of educators, there is an equal responsibility to provide them with the capacity to meet that expectation" (Elmore, 2004, p. 93). For example, principals of PLCs recognize that they have an obligation to provide staff members with the resources, training, mentoring, and support to help them successfully accomplish their goals.

Results orientation: A focus on outcomes rather than inputs or intentions. In PLCs, members are committed to achieving desired results and are hungry for evidence that their efforts are producing the intended outcomes.

Roger Bannister moment: In this book, the Roger Bannister moment references the engagement that occurs when a team (or member of a team) observes extraordinary results that lead to higher expectations and a willingness to seek new levels of performance.

S

Sacred time: Providing time for educators to engage in the essential work of the PLC process is a prerequisite for successful implementation of that process. Sacred time means that time set aside for educators to engage in the work will not be preempted for other purposes.

School culture: The assumptions, beliefs, expectations, values, and habits that constitute the norm for a school and guide the work of the educators within it. *Culture* has been defined as simply "the way we do things around here."

Servant leadership: A theory and practice of leadership wherein a leader works with others to establish a shared sense of purpose, goals, and direction and then creates the conditions to help them succeed at what they are trying to accomplish.

Shared goals: The specific targets and time lines established by a team in agreed pursuit of a specific result.

Shared knowledge: Members of PLCs attempt to answer critical questions by first learning together. They engage in collective inquiry to build shared knowledge. This collective study of the same information increases the likelihood that members arrive at the same conclusion. Members of a PLC, by definition, learn together.

Singleton: A term used to describe an educator who is the only person in his or her school assigned to teach a particular grade level or course. This makes the process of collaboration difficult in that the teacher is working alone.

Situational leadership: A theory and practice of leadership wherein a leader adapts his or her leadership style to the group, situation, and desired outcomes. It is based on the belief that there is not one "best" style of leadership but that each situation and group calls for different strategies of leading (Hersey & Blanchard, 1969).

SMART goals: Goals that are strategic and specific, measurable, attainable, results oriented, and time bound (Conzemius & O'Neill, 2014).

Stretch goals: Goals intended to inspire, capture the imagination of people within an organization, stimulate creativity and innovation, and serve as a unifying focal point of effort. Stretch goals are so ambitious that they typically cannot be achieved without significant changes in practice. Stretch goals are also referred to as *BHAGs: Big Hairy Audacious Goals* (Collins & Porras, 1997).

Synchronous learning and communication: A process that transfers knowledge and ideas among individuals or groups within the barriers of time and space. Participants must access conversations and lessons in real time, limiting reflection and think time to the present moment.

Systems of intervention and enrichment: A schoolwide plan that ensures every student in every course or grade level receives additional time and support for learning as soon as he or she experiences difficulty in acquiring essential knowledge and skills. Multitiered intervention occurs during the school day, and students are required, rather than invited, to devote the extra time and secure the extra support for learning. Systematic intervention means that what happens when a student does not learn is no longer left to the individual teacher to determine but is addressed according to a systematic plan.

T

Team: A team is a group of people who work interdependently to achieve a shared goal for which there is mutual accountability.

Team learning process: The cyclical process in which all teams in a PLC engage to stay focused on student learning. The team learning process includes clarifying the essential student learning (skills, concepts, and dispositions) for each unit of instruction; agreeing on the length of time devoted to a unit; developing multiple common formative assessments aligned with each essential outcome; establishing specific target scores or benchmarks necessary to demonstrate proficiency; analyzing common assessment results; and identifying and implementing improvement strategies. Teams address each step in the process by first building shared knowledge rather than pooling opinions.

Team norms: Collective commitments developed by each team to guide members in working together. Norms help team members clarify expectations regarding how they will work together to achieve their shared goals.

Technophiles: People who are enthusiastic about new technology.

Technophobes: People who avoid, dislike, or fear new technology.

Threaded discussions: A threaded discussion is an interaction that occurs in a virtual collaboration/discussion space wherein commentary is posted and follow-up commentary is added. The term *thread* is used because, as the conversation emerges, most learning management systems (LMSs) represent these discussions in what appears to be a weaving thread down the screens of the users. Threaded conversations offer a written history of dialogue and interaction regarding any idea debated or discussed.

V

Values (shared/collective commitments): The specific attitudes, behaviors, and collective commitments that must be demonstrated in order to advance the organization's vision. Articulated values answer the question, How must we behave in order to make our shared vision a reality? See also **collective commitments**.

Vertical teaming/collaboration: Collaborative efforts that involve team members from multiple grade levels. A K–12 mathematics team is an example of a vertical team. A K–5 elementary education team could also be considered vertical.

Virtual collaboration: Collaborative efforts that embrace the essence of what is required for true face-to-face collaboration and use technology to enhance this essential learning dynamic. Virtual collaboration is intended to ensure that the work online truly does represent the collaborative work of a team.

Virtual teaming: For the purposes of this book, *virtual teaming* is a term for describing the strategic approaches required for encouraging a team to use technology in a thoughtful and strategic way to work interdependently to achieve shared goals for which members are mutually accountable. Virtual teams not only require thoughtful adherence to what it means to be a team, they also must make thoughtful use of technology to embrace and, in some cases, enhance the power and potential of teams.

Vision: A realistic, credible, attractive future for an organization. Vision answers the question, What do we hope to become at some point in the future?

PLCs at Work™ and Virtual Collaboration: On the Tipping Point of Transformation
© 2016 Solution Tree Press • solution-tree.com • Visit **go.solution-tree.com/PLCbooks** to download this page.

References and Resources

Achterman, D., & Loertscher, D. V. (2008). Where in the role are you anyway? *CSLA Journal, 31*(2), 10–13.

Adams, H. (2008). *The education of Henry Adams.* Blacksburg, VA: Wilder.

Amabile, T., & Kramer, S. (2011). *The progress principle: Using small wins to ignite joy, engagement, and creativity at work.* Boston: Harvard Business Review Press.

Atkeson, S. (2014, November 11). Teachers' knowledge of technology undersold, study says [Blog post]. *Education Week.* Accessed at http://blogs.edweek.org/edweek/DigitalEducation /2014/11/teachers_more_tech-savvy_students.html on March 15, 2015.

Baker, E. L., Barton, P. E., Darling-Hammond, L., Haertel, E., Ladd, H. F., Linn, R. L., et al. (2010, August). *Problems with the use of student test scores to evaluate teachers* (Economic Policy Institute Briefing Paper No. 278). Washington, DC: Economic Policy Institute.

Baker, E. L., Gearhart, M., & Herman, J. L. (1994). Evaluating the Apple classrooms of tomorrow. In E. L. Baker & H. F. O'Neil Jr. (Eds.), *Technology assessment in education and training* (pp. 173–198). New York: Routledge.

Barber, M., & Mourshed, M. (2007, September). *How the world's best-performing school systems come out on top.* New York: McKinsey & Company. Accessed at http://mckinseyonsociety .com/downloads/reports/Education/Worlds_School_Systems _Final.pdf on February 3, 2015.

Barber, M., & Mourshed, M. (2009, July). *Shaping the future: How good education systems can become great in the decade ahead* (Report on the International Education Roundtable). New York: McKinsey & Company.

Barth, R. S. (2001). *Learning by heart.* San Francisco: Jossey-Bass.

BBC Online. (1954, May 6). *Bannister breaks four-minute mile.* Accessed at http://news.bbc.co.uk/onthisday/hi/dates/stories /may/6/newsid_2511000/2511575.stm on March 15, 2015.

Berry, L. L., & Seltman, K. D. (2008). *Management lessons from Mayo Clinic: Inside one of the world's most admired service organizations.* New York: McGraw-Hill.

Blanchard, K. (2007). *Leading at a higher level: Blanchard on leadership and creating high performing organizations.* Upper Saddle River, NJ: Pearson/Prentice Hall.

Blanchard, K., Cuff, K., & Halsey, V. (2014). *Legendary service: The key is to care.* New York: McGraw-Hill.

Bonk, C. J. (2009). *The world is open: How web technology is revolutionizing education.* San Francisco: Jossey-Bass.

Bonk, C. J. (2010). For openers: How technology is changing school. *Educational Leadership, 67*(7), 60–65.

Boss, S. (2015). Powering up learning with PBL plus technology. In J. A. Bellanca (Ed.), *Deeper learning: Beyond 21st century skills* (pp. 111–135). Bloomington, IN: Solution Tree Press.

Burstein, D. D. (2013). *Fast future: How the millennial generation is shaping our world.* Boston: Beacon Press.

Byrom, E., & Bingham, M. (2001). *Factors influencing the effective use of technology for teaching and learning: Lessons learned from the SEIR-TEC intensive site schools* (2nd ed.). Durham, NC: SEIR-TEC. Accessed at http://ftp.serve.org/seir-tec/publications/lessons.pdf on February 2, 2015.

Carroll, T. (2009). The next generation of learning teams. *Phi Delta Kappan, 91*(2), 8–13.

Chandler, D. L. (2012, May 2). MIT and Harvard launch a 'revolution in education.' *MIT News*. Accessed at http://newsoffice.mit.edu/2012/edx-launched-0502 on February 2, 2015.

Collins, J. (2001). *Good to great: Why some companies make the leap . . . and others don't*. New York: HarperBusiness.

Collins, J., & Porras, J. I. (1997). *Built to last: Successful habits of visionary companies*. New York: HarperBusiness.

Conzemius, A. E., & O'Neill, J. (2014). *The Handbook for SMART school teams: Revitalizing best practices for collaboration* (2nd ed.). Bloomington, IN: Solution Tree Press.

Covey, S. R. (2013). *The 7 habits of highly effective people: Powerful lessons in personal change* (25th anniversary ed.). New York: Simon & Schuster.

Covey, S. R., Merrill, A. R., & Merrill, R. R. (1995). *First things first*. New York: Simon & Schuster.

Cuban, L. (1993). Computers meet classroom: Classroom wins. *Teachers College Record, 95*(2), 185–210.

Cuban, L. (2001). *Oversold and underused: Computers in the classroom*. Cambridge, MA: Harvard University Press.

Cubberley, E. P. (1919). *Public education in the United States: A study and interpretation of American educational history*. Boston: Houghton Mifflin.

Darling-Hammond, L., Barron, B., Pearson, P. D., Schoenfeld, A. H., Stage, E. K., Zimmerman, T. D., et al. (2008). *Powerful learning: What we know about teaching for understanding.* San Francisco: Jossey-Bass.

David, J. L., & Talbert, J. E. (2013). *Turning around a high-poverty district: Learning from Sanger.* San Francisco: S. H. Cowell Foundation.

Deming, W. E. (n.d.). *The fourteen points for management.* Accessed at https://www.deming.org/theman/theories/fourteenpoints on February 2, 2015.

Digenti, D. (1999). Collaborative learning: A core capability for organizations in the new economy. *Reflections, 1*(2), 45–57.

DuFour, R., DuFour, R., & Eaker, R. (2008). *Revisiting Professional Learning Communities at Work: New insights for improving schools.* Bloomington, IN: Solution Tree Press.

DuFour, R., DuFour, R., Eaker, R., & Many, T. (2010). *Learning by doing: A handbook for Professional Learning Communities at Work* (2nd ed.). Bloomington, IN: Solution Tree Press.

DuFour, R., Eaker, R., & DuFour, R. (2007). *The power of Professional Learning Communities at Work: Bringing the big ideas to life.* Bloomington, IN: Solution Tree Press.

DuFour, R., & Fullan, M. (2013). *Cultures built to last: Systemic PLCs at Work.* Bloomington, IN: Solution Tree Press.

DuFour, R., & Marzano, R. J. (2011). *Leaders of learning: How district, school, and classroom leaders improve student achievement.* Bloomington, IN: Solution Tree Press.

Ebrahim, N. A., Ahmed, S., & Taha, Z. (2009). Virtual teams: A literature review. *Australian Journal of Basic and Applied Sciences, 3*(3), 2653–2669.

Elmore, R. F. (2004). *School reform from the inside out: Policy, practice, and performance.* Cambridge, MA: Harvard Education Press.

Ferguson, R. F., Hackman, S., Hanna, R., & Ballantine, A. (2010, June). *How high schools become exemplary: Ways that leadership raises achievement and narrows gaps by improving instruction in 15 public high schools* (Report on the 2009 Annual Conference of the Achievement Gap Initiative at Harvard University). Accessed at www.agi.harvard.edu/events/2009Conference /2009AGIConferenceReport6-30-2010web.pdf on February 2, 2015.

Friedman, T. L. (2005). *The world is flat: A brief history of the twenty-first century.* New York: Farrar, Straus and Giroux.

Fullan, M. (2005). *Leadership and sustainability: System thinkers in action.* Thousand Oaks, CA: Corwin Press.

Fullan, M. (2013). The new pedagogy: Students and teachers as learning partners. *LEARNing Landscapes, 6*(2), 23–29.

Fullan, M. (2014). *The principal: Three keys to maximizing impact.* San Francisco: Jossey-Bass.

Fulton, K., & Britton, T. (2011, June). *STEM teachers in professional learning communities: From good teachers to great teaching.* Washington, DC: National Commission on Teaching and America's Future.

Gallimore, R., Ermeling, B. A., Saunders, W. M., & Goldenberg, C. (2009). Moving the learning of teaching closer to practice: Teacher education implications of school-based inquiry teams. *Elementary School Journal, 109*(5), 537–553.

Gardner, J. W. (1990). *On leadership.* New York: Free Press.

Gladwell, M. (2002). *The tipping point: How little things can make a big difference.* Boston: Back Bay Books.

Goleman, D., Boyatzis, R., & McKee, A. (2004). *Primal leadership: Learning to lead with emotional intelligence.* Boston: Harvard Business School Press.

Hargreaves, A., & Fullan, M. (2012). *Professional capital: Transforming teaching in every school.* New York: Teachers College Press.

Hattie, J. (2009). *Visible learning: A synthesis of over 800 meta-analyses relating to achievement.* New York: Routledge.

Hattie, J. (2012). *Visible learning for teachers: Maximizing impact on learning.* New York: Routledge.

Heath, C., & Heath, D. (2010). *Switch: How to change things when change is hard.* New York: Broadway Books.

Hersey, P., & Blanchard, K. H. (1969). *Management of organizational behavior: Utilizing human resources.* Englewood Cliffs, NJ: Prentice Hall.

Higgins, S., Xiao, Z., & Katsipataki, M. (2012, November). *The impact of digital technology on learning: A summary for the Education Endowment Foundation.* London: Education Endowment Foundation. Accessed at https://larrycuban.files .wordpress.com/2013/12/the_impact_of_digital_technologies _on_learning_full_report_2012.pdf on April 16, 2015.

Hopkins, J., & Turner, J. (2012). *Go mobile: Location-based marketing, apps, mobile optimized ad campaigns, 2D codes, and other mobile strategies to grow your business.* Hoboken, NJ: Wiley.

Howe, J. (2009). *Crowdsourcing: Why the power of the crowd is driving the future of business.* New York: Three Rivers Press.

Howe, N., & Strauss, W. (2000). *Millennials rising: The next great generation.* New York: Vintage Books.

Johnson, S. M., & Kardos, S. M. (2004). Professional culture and the promise of colleagues. In S. M. Johnson & the Project on the Next Generation of Teachers, *Finders and keepers: Helping new teachers survive and thrive in our schools* (pp. 139–166). San Francisco: Jossey-Bass.

Kanter, R. M. (2004). *Confidence: How winning streaks and losing streaks begin and end.* New York: Crown Business.

Katzenbach, J. R., & Smith, D. K. (1993). *The wisdom of teams: Creating the high-performance organization*. Boston: Harvard Business School Press.

Kegan, R., & Lahey, L. L. (2001). *How the way we talk can change the way we work: Seven languages for transformation*. San Francisco: Jossey-Bass.

Kirkman, B. L., Rosen, B., Gibson, C. B., Tesluk, P. E., & McPherson, S. O. (2002). Five challenges to virtual team success: Lessons from Sabre, Inc. *Academy of Management Executive, 16*(3), 67–79.

Kotter, J. P. (1996). *Leading change*. Boston: Harvard Business School Press.

Kouzes, J. M., & Posner, B. Z. (2003). *Encouraging the heart: A leader's guide to rewarding and recognizing others*. San Francisco: Jossey-Bass.

Learning Forward. (n.d.). *Standards for professional learning*. Accessed at http://learningforward.org/standards/learning-communities#.VJ1x2CnAA on February 2, 2015.

Lencioni, P. (2005). *Overcoming the five dysfunctions of a team: A field guide for leaders, managers, and facilitators*. San Francisco: Jossey-Bass.

Little, J. W. (2006, December). *Professional community and professional development in the learning-centered school*. Washington, DC: National Education Association. Accessed at www.nea.org/assets/docs/HE/mf_pdreport.pdf on February 2, 2015.

Little, J. W., & Bartlett, L. (2010). The teacher workforce and problems of educational equity. *Review of Research in Education, 34*(1), 285–328.

Louis, K. S., & Wahlstrom, K. (2011). Principals as cultural leaders. *Phi Delta Kappan, 92*(5), 52–56.

Marzano, R. J. (2003). *What works in schools: Translating research into action*. Alexandria: VA: Association for Supervision and Curriculum Development.

Marzano, R. J. (2009). Setting the record straight on "high-yield" strategies. *Phi Delta Kappan, 91*(1), 30–37.

Marzano, R. J., Waters, T., & McNulty, B. A. (2005). *School leadership that works: From research to results*. Alexandria, VA: Association for Supervision and Curriculum Development.

Mayo Clinic. (2014). *Mayo Clinic model of care*. Jacksonville, FL: Author. Accessed at www.mayo.edu/pmts/mc4200-mc4299/mc4270.pdf on February 2, 2015.

McLaughlin, M. W., & Talbert, J. E. (2006). *Building school-based teacher learning communities: Professional strategies to improve student achievement*. New York: Teachers College Press.

Meyer, E. (2010, August 19). The four keys to success with virtual teams. *Forbes*. Accessed at www.forbes.com/2010/08/19/virtual-teams-meetings-leadership-managing-cooperation.html on February 27, 2015.

Michelangelo. (n.d.). *Michelangelo quotes*. Accessed at www.brainyquote.com/quotes/quotes/m/michelange108779.html on February 2, 2015.

Mourshed, M., Chijioke, C., & Barber, M. (2010, November). *How the world's most improved school systems keep getting better*. New York: McKinsey & Company. Accessed at http://mckinseyonsociety.com/how-the-worlds-most-improved-school-systems-keep-getting-better on February 2, 2015.

Newmann, F. M., & associates. (1996). *Authentic achievement: Restructuring schools for intellectual quality*. San Francisco: Jossey-Bass.

Organisation for Economic Co-operation and Development. (2014a). *Key findings from the Teaching and Learning International Survey (TALIS) 2013: United States of America.* Paris: Author. Accessed at www.oecd.org/unitedstates/TALIS -2013-country-note-US.pdf on February 4, 2015.

Organisation for Economic Co-operation and Development. (2014b). *Teaching and Learning International Survey 2013 results: An international perspective on teaching and learning.* Paris: Author.

Partnership for 21st Century Skills. (n.d.a). *21st century learning environments.* Accessed at www.p21.org/about-us/p21 -framework/354 on February 2, 2015.

Partnership for 21st Century Skills. (n.d.b). *21st century professional development.* Accessed at www.p21.org/about-us /p21-framework/831 on February 2, 2015.

Partnership for 21st Century Skills. (n.d.c). *Communication and collaboration.* Accessed at www.p21.org/about-us/p21 -framework/261 on February 2, 2015.

Passeri, P. (2015, January 13). *2014 cyber attacks statistics (aggregated).* Accessed at www.hackmageddon.com/2015/01/13/2014 -cyber-attacks-statistics-aggregated on June 29, 2015.

Patterson, K., Grenny, J., Maxfield, D., McMillan, R., & Switzler, A. (2008). *Influencer: The power to change anything.* New York: McGraw-Hill.

Pearson, K. (1930). *The life, letters and labours of Francis Galton* (Vol. 3a). Cambridge, England: Cambridge University Press.

Perkins, D. (2003). *King Arthur's round table: How collaborative conversations create smart organizations.* Hoboken, NJ: Wiley.

Pew Research Center Internet Project. (2014). *Social networking fact sheet.* Accessed at www.pewinternet.org/fact-sheets/social -networking-fact-sheet on December 12, 2014.

Pink, D. H. (2009). *Drive: The surprising truth about what motivates us.* New York: Riverhead Books.

Proust, M. (n.d.). *Quotes.* Accessed at www.goodreads.com/author /quotes/233619.Marcel_Proust on March 9, 2015.

Reeves, D. B. (2011). *Finding your leadership focus: What matters most for student results.* New York: Teachers College Press.

Robers, S., Kemp, J., Rathbun, A., Morgan, R. E., & Snyder, T. D. (2014, June). *Indicators of school crime and safety: 2013* (NCES 2014-042). Washington, DC: National Center for Education Statistics, U.S. Department of Education. Accessed at http:// nces.ed.gov/pubs2014/2014042.pdf on April 16, 2015.

RW³ CultureWizard. (2010). *The challenges of working in virtual teams: Virtual teams survey report—2010.* New York: Author. Accessed at http://rw-3.com/VTSReportv7.pdf on February 2, 2015.

Saphier, J., King, M., & D'Auria, J. (2006). Three strands form strong school leadership. *Journal of Staff Development, 27*(2), 51–57.

Sarason, S. B. (1996). *Revisiting "the culture of the school and the problem of change."* New York: Teachers College Press.

Schlechty, P. C. (1997). *Inventing better schools: An action plan for educational reform.* San Francisco: Jossey-Bass.

Schmoker, M. (2004). Tipping point: From feckless reform to substantive instructional improvement. *Phi Delta Kappan, 85*(6), 424–432.

Schrum, L. (Ed.). (2010). *Considerations on technology and teachers: The best of JRTE.* Eugene, OR: International Society for Technology in Education.

Schwartz, K. (2013, February 13). *Are teachers of tomorrow prepared to use innovative tech?* Accessed at ww2.kqed.org /mindshift/2013/02/13/are-teachers-of-tomorrow-prepared -to-use-innovative-tech on April 16, 2015.

Senge, P., Kleiner, A., Roberts, C., Ross, R., & Smith, B. (1994). *The fifth discipline fieldbook: Strategies and tools for building a learning organization.* New York: Currency/Doubleday.

Shermis, M. D., & Burstein, J. (Eds.). (2013). *Handbook of automated essay evaluation: Current applications and new directions.* New York: Routledge.

Sparks, S. D. (2014, June 25). *Survey: Teachers worldwide seek more opportunities for collaboration* [Blog post]. Accessed at http:// blogs.edweek.org/edweek/inside-school-research/2014/06 /teachers_worldwide_seek_more_c.html?cmp=ENL-EU -NEWS2 on February 2, 2015.

Taylor, F. W. (1911). *The principles of scientific management.* New York: Harper & Brothers.

Tehrani, K., & Michael, A. (2014, March 26). Wearable technology and wearable devices: Everything you need to know. *Wearable Devices Magazine.* Accessed at www .wearabledevices.com/what-is-a-wearable-device on February 2, 2015.

Thimmesh, C. (2006). *Team moon: How 400,000 people landed Apollo 11 on the moon.* New York: Houghton Mifflin.

Timperley, H. S., & Robinson, V. M. J. (2001). Achieving school improvement through challenging and changing teachers' schema. *Journal of Educational Change, 2*(4), 281–300.

Tu, C.-H., & Corry, M. (2003). Building active online interaction via a collaborative learning community. *Computers in the Schools, 20*(3), 51–59.

Tyack, D., & Cuban, L. (1995). *Tinkering toward utopia: A century of public school reform.* Cambridge, MA: Harvard University Press.

U.S. Bureau of the Census. (1991). *Statistical abstract of the United States, 1991* (111th ed.). Washington, DC: Author.

U.S. Bureau of the Census. (2001). *Statistical abstract of the United States, 1995–2000*. Washington, DC: Author.

Van Dusen, G. C. (1997). The virtual campus: Technology and reform in higher education. *ASHE-ERIC Higher Education Report, 25*(5). Washington, DC: George Washington University Graduate School of Education and Human Development.

Wallace Foundation. (2012, January). *The school principal as leader: Guiding schools to better teaching and learning*. New York: Author. Accessed at www.wallacefoundation.org/knowledge -center/school-leadership/effective-principal-leadership /Documents/The-School-Principal-as-Leader-Guiding-Schools -to-Better-Teaching-and-Learning.pdf on February 2, 2015.

Waterman, R. H., Jr. (1993). *Adhocracy*. New York: Norton.

Watkins, M. (2013, June 27). Making virtual teams work: Ten basic principles. *Harvard Business Review*. Accessed at https:// hbr.org/2013/06/making-virtual-teams-work-ten on February 2, 2015.

Wenglinsky, H. (1998, September). *Does it compute?: The relationship between educational technology and student achievement in mathematics*. Princeton, NJ: Educational Testing Service Policy Information Center.

Index

Solutions for Digital Learner–Centered Classrooms series

With a short, reader-friendly format, these quick reads deliver practical, high-impact 21st century strategies to enhance instruction and heighten student achievement.

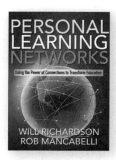

Personal Learning Networks
Will Richardson and Rob Mancabelli

Follow this road map for using the web for learning. Use learning networks in the classroom and schoolwide to improve student outcomes.

BKF484

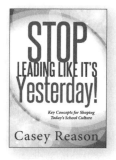

Stop Leading Like It's Yesterday!
Casey Reason

Explore the Leading for Excellence and Fulfillment model, and discover practical, research-based strategies that are relevant to school leaders today and tomorrow.

BKF614

Revisiting Professional Learning Communities at Work™
Richard DuFour, Rebecca DuFour, and Robert Eaker

This tenth-anniversary sequel to *Professional Learning Communities at Work™* offers advanced insights on deep implementation, the commitment/consensus issue, and the human side of PLCs.

BKF252

Solution Tree | Press

a division of

Solution Tree

Visit solution-tree.com or call 800.733.6786 to order.

Wait! Your professional development journey doesn't have to end with the last pages of this book.

We realize improving student learning doesn't happen overnight. And your school or district shouldn't be left to puzzle out all the details of this process alone.

No matter where you are on the journey, we're committed to helping you get to the next stage.

Take advantage of everything from **custom workshops** to **keynote presentations** and **interactive web and video conferencing**. We can even help you develop an action plan tailored to fit your specific needs.

Let's get the conversation started.

Call 888.763.9045 today.

solution-tree.com

Solution Tree

Solution Tree's mission is to advance the work of our authors. By working with the best researchers and educators worldwide, we strive to be the premier provider of innovative publishing, in-demand events, and inspired professional development designed to transform education to ensure that all students learn.

Great Public Schools for Every Student

Our mission is to advocate for education professionals and to unite our members and the nation to fulfill the promise of public education to prepare every student to succeed in a diverse and interdependent world.